WILLIAMSBURG
A CITY THAT HISTORY MADE

Late nineteenth-century Williamsburg on a summer's day looking west from what was then called Capitol Green. (Courtesy Visual Resources Center, John D. Rockefeller Library, Colonial Williamsburg, Inc.)

THE MAKING OF AMERICA

WILLIAMSBURG
A CITY THAT HISTORY MADE

TIMOTHY E. MORGAN

ARCADIA

Copyright © 2004 by Timothy E. Morgan.
ISBN 0-7385-2473-5

Published by Arcadia Publishing,
Charleston SC, Chicago IL, Portsmouth NH, San Francisco CA

Printed in Great Britain.

Library of Congress Catalog Card Number: 2004112097

For all general information contact Arcadia Publishing at:
Telephone 843-853-2070
Fax 843-853-0044
E-Mail sales@arcadiapublishing.com
For customer service and orders:
Toll-Free 1-888-313-2665

Visit us on the Internet at http://www.arcadiapublishing.com

CONTENTS

ACKNOWLEDGMENTS

This project could not have been produced without the kind and encouraging help of several people. Amy Boykin, Reference Librarian at Christopher Newport University, has been unfailingly helpful in finding materials for the project. Marianne Martin and Laura Arnette of the Visual Resources Center at the John D. Rockefeller Library of the Colonial Williamsburg Foundation were also extremely kind and helpful providing assistance in the selection of visual images for this work.

Alain and Merry Abbitt Outlaw and Mary Clemons of Archaeological and Cultural Solutions, Incorporated, provided substantial assistance in assessing the importance of archaeology and recommending visuals to illustrate prehistoric occupation near Williamsburg. My wife, Michele McMurtry, deserves special recognition for putting up with the author during the time spent researching and writing this book.

The author and author alone is responsible for any and all errors of fact or interpretation contained within the covers of this work.

INTRODUCTION

The City of Williamsburg and several of the institutions that comprise important portions of it (such as The College of William and Mary or Bruton Parish Church or Eastern State Hospital) have long histories. Many of those institutions have good or excellent accounts of them. The restoration, getting close to eighty years old, also has many well-done histories. A general narrative of the city can bring those accounts and others like them together, for the history of the city of Williamsburg is history. The town has a unique niche in American history. It made an impact in the eighteenth century as Virginia's colonial capital and one of the cockpits of the American Revolution. The political figures inhabiting the capital in the Revolutionary era understood the city's wealth and power, and the fact that those two derived from the large population and great wealth of the colony itself. Virginia laid claim to all the land west to the Mississippi River, north of the Virginia–North Carolina boundary, and northwest from the mouth of the Potomac River to the Great Lakes—a territory the size of many European nations at the time. The power the city's imperial and colonial leaders exerted stretched well beyond the colony's borders in the First British Empire.

With transfer of Virginia's capital from Williamsburg to Richmond in 1780, the town stagnated, declined, and entered a long sleep. The restoration, funded by John D. Rockefeller Jr., began in 1926. History revived the city, the restoration making it a symbol of American principles of freedom, liberty, individualism, and self-government. For almost eighty years Williamsburg has come to symbolize to many Americans what they think their forefathers stood for and meant. The city has become an intellectual and cultural center in which intense discussions of that meaning have taken and continue to take place.

This book is a general exploration of Williamsburg's past, highlighting how history has made the city and what that has meant for it. Images of the town and some of its residents speak to its annals and its eccentricities, for when it was a sleepy little southern town, it was eccentric. Williamsburg has had a direct experience with warfare, probably more so than most American cities and towns. Every war in which the United States has fought, Williamsburg has done its share in providing soldiers and support. The city has shared with the nation the long agony of slavery and its racial legacies. In sum, Williamsburg has participated in and witnessed, or even directed, much history. It is to that process by which history has made the city that this work is directed.

Chapter One

BEGINNINGS

The city of Williamsburg today is the historical product of thousands, perhaps even millions, of years of physical change and natural and cultural evolution. The city, located on the ridge running the length of the peninsula formed by the James and York Rivers and the Chesapeake Bay, sits just outside the rim of the sixth-largest meteorite-formed crater on the face of the earth. The geology and geography of Williamsburg are the product of millions of years of slow change punctuated by at least two major catastrophic periods: a meteorite impact 35 million years ago and the end of the last ice age when the earth's water levels rose dramatically.

The meteorite struck near what is today Cape Charles, the small town at the southern tip of the Eastern Shore peninsula. It was about two to three miles wide, entered earth's atmosphere traveling about 60,000 miles per hour, and hit with the force of 10 trillion tons of dynamite. The region was under about 600 feet of water then and the impact threw up not only massive quantities of ash, dust, and other debris, but similar quantities of water, creating vast tsunamis reaching as far as the Appalachian mountains. Today the crater rim lies just a few miles east and several hundred feet below ground level of Williamsburg, and the city itself rests on the ejecta blanket (the great quantity of dust, ash, and other debris thrown out of the crater).

The Chesapeake Bay and its tributary rivers thus are a geological part of that great catastrophe. But the bay itself came into existence just 12,000 years ago when the earth began warming at the end of the last Ice Age. Water levels rose dramatically for the next 3,000 years and the bay and its tributaries took on their modern form. Meteorite-created breccia, a mix of rocks and small dirt particles that sank comparatively faster than lands outside the crater rim, filled the south end of the bay (the crater). As a result, the James and York Rivers, which reach the bay after they cross the rim, have turned about ninety degrees to the left (roughly northeast) before entering the bay. The Potomac and Rappahannock Rivers, the two other major Virginia tributaries to the north, follow their northwest to southeast courses as they enter the bay, for their mouths lie well outside the crater's rim.

One other important geological fact concerning the Williamsburg area is that local water levels are rising at about the fastest rate in the world during this current period of global warming. Geologists think that breccia subsidence, rather than global warming, explains the water level rise. Since the meteorite's impact, some 300 feet of clay and sand, plus other sediments, have covered the breccia and ejecta layers, creating the clayey-sandy soils of the peninsula. Since bedrock lies some 2,300 feet below surface, compaction of the bay's breccia and clayey-sandy soils occurs more easily than in geologic areas where bedrock comes closer to the surface.

Until water levels started rising about 12,000 years ago, tributary rivers were little more than creeks or streams. The bay did not exist; it was today's Susquehanna River that turned east and flowed across what is now the continental shelf, until it finally reached the ocean about 200 miles to the east of the current shoreline. Only when the Earth warmed did water levels rise, creating the bay and deepening the tributaries to the point that today the James River, for instance, is about 4.3 miles wide at the James River Bridge.

As the earth warmed, the climate of the region shifted from boreal to warm temperate. Deciduous hardwoods (oak and hickory especially) mixed with conifers in vast forests. Marshes, bogs, swamps, and shallows formed along the rivers as water levels rose. A wide variety of fish, shellfish, water grasses and other water plants, land animals, and land plants settled in the bay area, making a rich and attractive habitat for predators, including humans. Archaeologists working in western Virginia found campsites dating to 10,000 years ago, but the earliest sites for the Williamsburg area date to approximately 2,500 years ago. One site, currently being excavated, dates to between 1,000 and 2,000 years ago. Some scholars, however, think that the James or York Rivers cover many campsites dating to earlier times.

The earliest human inhabitants of the Americas arrived at the latest 12,000 years ago, although much evidence indicates it was much earlier, perhaps 25,000 years ago. They crossed a subcontinental-sized landmass called Beringia, where today the Bering Strait exists. These early humans (Paleolithic or Old Stone Age peoples) hunted large mammals such as the woolly mammoth, mastodons, and giant bison. Once the great ice caps created during the last Ice Age began to melt, unblocking paths southward from modern Alaska, these late Paleolithic peoples migrated rapidly. These hunter-gatherers may have arrived at the southern tip of South America within 1,000 years after leaving Alaska, but their wanderings brought them to the Virginia region by about 10,000 years ago.

Thousands of years passed between the arrival of the first Paleo-Indians and the development of Eastern Woodlands culture. Many generations of Stone Age peoples lived and flourished in Virginia before Europeans invaded in the late sixteenth and early seventeenth centuries. Paleolithic peoples passed through many cultural changes, but the most important was the shift to vegetable agriculture. Between 7,000 and 5,000 years ago peoples in Central and South America domesticated maize (corn) and potatoes respectively, beginning the Neolithic era. Over time, Neolithic farmers domesticated many other species of plant foods like tomatoes, many varieties of beans and peppers, squashes and pumpkins, sunflowers, and tobacco after they learned the basic rules for domesticating plants. Slowly, knowledge of such agriculture passed by what anthropologists call cultural diffusion into the modern-day southeastern United States. Centuries before Europeans came to settle, Indians in the eastern region of North America had adopted vegetable agriculture of corn, beans, and squashes to their needs. North American natives, however, had no domesticable animals except the dog. They raised turkeys and some other fowl as well. Although excellent horticulturists, they had to depend on hunting, fishing, and trapping for meat and fish.

When Europeans came to this veritable cornucopia in eastern Virginia, there lived an empire of Native Americans called the Powhatan Chieftainship. Led by a "paramount chief," there existed some thirty separate people or tribes (the terms are used interchangeably) united, however weakly, under his control in a triple-tiered system. The farther from the center of the empire one went geographically, the weaker the chief's control. Powhatan himself comprised the first tier. The second tier—lesser chiefs called weroances who were usually his male relatives or close friends through whom he ruled—lived in and controlled the various villages or tribes of the empire. Leaders of small villages and towns of each separate tribe comprised the third and bottom tier. Although the Powhatan peoples had no written language, they did possess a code of laws and prescriptions concerning proper conduct within the villages, among the villages, and with outsiders.

These native peoples with whom sixteenth-century European intruders came in contact had a well-developed, neolithic way of life. Relying on the rich environment of the Chesapeake Bay, the Powhatan chiefdom extended from the south side of the James River north to the Potomac, and from the fall line to the Eastern Shore. With an estimated 15,000 to 35,000 people (depending on the scholar) included in the chiefdom, the Powhatans had a rich, developed culture.

A semi-sedentary people, the Powhatans lived in villages located along riverbanks and streambeds. They regarded rivers as central highways of transportation, as unifiers of a people. Europeans, on the other hand, thought of rivers as political and cultural boundaries. The Powhatans built large log canoes to use on their principal highways for hunting, fishing, transit of trade goods and people, and to make war. Powhatans used rivers, streams, wetlands, and the bay as important parts of their livelihood.

Williamsburg

The Chesapeake Bay's tributary rivers are brackish from the bay to the fall line, depending on the season. During fall, winter, and spring the rivers contain much higher levels of fresh water than in summer. In summer, generally a drier season than the others, salt content rises in the rivers. This brackish variability made for good breeding grounds for migratory fish such as sturgeon or shad, and excellent places for oysters and clams to reproduce in the rivers. Crabs also teemed in the rivers. Migratory waterfowl such as Canadian geese and a wide variety of ducks came to the rivers and bay to winter as part of their annual migration pattern. Passenger pigeons and other extinct birds and animals migrated to or lived along the river drainages as well.

The heart of the Powhatan chiefdom lived near the conjunction of the James and Appomattox Rivers and the paramount chief, titled Powhatan but named Wahunsenacawh, ruled from his capital at Werowocomoco on the north bank of the York River when the English arrived in 1607. His people grew four varieties of maize, two types of pole beans, and various kinds of squashes and pumpkins in garden plots allotted to those wanting to use them. Women planted the corn and beans in small hills or mounds, spaced about four feet apart, which they worked up with wooden digging sticks. They first planted a few grains of corn in each hill, then a few beans. Once the corn began to grow, the beans could grow up around the cornstalks. Then they planted squashes and pumpkins in the spaces between the hillocks. The beans, being legumes, constantly replaced nitrogen the corn fed on, thus helping to fertilize the corn and maintain general fertility. The squashes and pumpkins, being leafy, helped keep the soil damp and cut down on weed growth. Anthropologists and archaeologists do not agree on just how much food these gardens supplied, but estimates vary between 40 and 60 percent of annual foodstuff production.

The Powhatans divided work by gender as men and women had their own spheres of labor in the villages. The Powhatans probably did not have to devote a large amount of their daily time to labor, maybe three to five hours. Children participated in production to aid with daily food gathering and to learn how to be an adult. They also learned what their people valued as adults. For instance, some Powhatan mothers refused to feed their sons in the mornings until the boys had demonstrated some skill such as bowmanship.

Men hunted, fished, and trapped, and women planted and tended the gardens and gathered a variety of wild plants for additional food, decorative uses, and medicines. Wild foods gathered included various kinds of nuts (such as acorns, black walnuts, and hickory), roots such as tuckahoe, fruits like cherries and persimmons, and leafy plants. Although sixteenth- and seventeenth-century English interpreted Powhatan men's hunting and fishing as sport (what they knew them to be in Europe), native males worked at hunting, fishing, and trapping. Their families and villages depended on their ability to provide protein-rich meat and fish and raw materials (mostly deer hides and skins) for clothing. Males' status depended on their hunting and fishing abilities because Powhatan peoples measured wealth in food and the ability to provide it. If a young man proved himself a capable hunter, he could expect to win the woman of his choice when it came time to marry. Similarly, a young woman who proved competent at gardening and gathering could expect to win the affections of a good hunter.

Powhatan society was matriarchal and matrilineal. Since women remained in the villages and did the gardening/gathering and men left villages to hunt, fish, and make war, lines of descent passed through women rather than men. Powhatan's younger brothers inherited his mantle of authority when he died in 1618, not his eldest son. Powhatans had no concept of private real estate; the village communally owned the lands and those who needed plots for gardens or fields used them until they were through or the fields lost their nutrient strength. Then the fields reverted to the collective "pot" of land and the gardener or farmer moved to another patch to continue her production. The Powhatans had similar ideas about hunting lands; one village or people communally controlled their own hunting lands, but any hunter from the Powhatan group might enter those lands if pursuing game he had wounded or begun stalking elsewhere.

The Powhatan people lived in large, quonset-shaped longhouses. Built of saplings, handmade cordage, and mats, the houses maintained warmth in winters. The women constructed the housing, beginning with saplings that they stuck several inches into the ground in parallel lines about fifteen to twenty feet apart. Saplings also framed the gable ends of the longhouse. The parallel lines might be twenty to one hundred feet in length, depending on the number of families living in the new house. The women then bent the saplings over from each side and tied them together, creating an arbor-like framework. Once they completed the basic framework, they wove smaller saplings crosswise to strengthen it. Then they draped mats made from reeds or furs or tree bark on the sides. They left one or more smokeholes in the roof, depending on the number of people living in the house. A door was constructed at each end. The women built sleeping pallets about twelve to eighteen inches off the dirt floor, pallets that could be covered with furs or hides. From the cross-braces added within the house could be hung skins, drying corn, cooking pots, bows and arrows, spears, and tools for gardening. Women and men made the cordage, using soft bark and rolling it together into strands between the palms of their hands while they gripped it with their thighs to get a good tight weave. Cordage used to tie the house framework together was strong and long-lasting.

Williamsburg

The Powhatan built their villages in small clusters of longhouses, ten or fifteen at a time, usually on high ground overlooking an adjacent river or stream. The houses could hold six to forty people, usually all blood-related through women. Villages might contain 50, 250, 1,000, or perhaps even 3,000 persons, comparable to European villages and towns of the period. The towns' inhabitants worked daily for their food and clothing. They made clothing from skins and hides of animals killed for meat. After tanning a deerskin, it might be transformed into a breechclout for a man, a skirt for a woman, or moccasins and other footwear for anyone in the family. Women did the tanning and curing of hides and skins.

Powhatans made tools and weapons from stones, bones, horns, and wood. Everything from needles to awls, hammers, and axes was constructed of stone, bone, or wood. But Powhatan people had to rely more on bone, wood, and horn than other North American natives, since stone was in short supply in the Tidewater Virginia region. Before Europeans intruded into their homeland, Powhatans adapted many stone-working techniques to bone or wood or horn. Women made substantial cooking pots shaped to sit in their open fires. They also made many other types of pottery, all hand-made using a technique called "coil," in which the women rolled out long strands of pottery clay then rolled the coils into circles of varying diameter. They then stacked the coils one on top of the other, and used wood tools to shape the pot the way they wanted it before finishing it and firing it.

Their pottery, hammers, axes, awls, needles, fishhooks, and other tools and weapons served them well in their environment, but once European iron tools and weapons appeared in eastern Virginia in the sixteenth and seventeenth centuries, native men and women alike began to trade for them. Powhatans found not only European tools and weapons attractive; they found iron cooking pots and pans interesting too. Powhatan men and women embraced European trade goods to the extent that within three to four generations after English intrusion, the Powhatans lost many traditional stone-working and pottery-making skills.

A nonliterate people, the Powhatans transmitted their religious, political, social, and cultural beliefs orally. Older Powhatans watched young boys carefully to see who might demonstrate the memory and verbal qualifications to become religious or diplomatic leaders and spokesmen for the people. Those boys who gave evidence of such memories began training in the people's religion and history at a young age. Religious leaders, called shamans, possessed healing and religious knowledge. Powhatan religion was spirit-based. They believed that all living creatures and some non-living, too, had spirits whom they should supplicate. Shamans and other religious leaders were highly regarded and respected in their culture. Political leaders consulted them on important questions of war or public policy. Powhatans lived a collective life in which they had integrated their religion thoroughly.

Powhatans possessed a rich religion rooted in several gods, the most important of whom was Oke (Okeus, Okee, and other names). Oke was a stern and demanding god whom the seventeenth-century English equated with Satan, but he appears from English descriptions to resemble more the Old Testament Jehovah than Satan. Powhatans had a creation story and identified various spirits with important portions of their lives, such as hunting, fishing, and agriculture. They bathed every morning when they awoke, in a freshwater stream or pond, following which they prayed to their gods. They regarded bathing as part of their religious observance. Babies and children likewise bathed each morning, no matter the temperature. Such activity hardened and inured the children to the rigors of their life. Europeans consistently commented on Powhatans' ability to withstand the harshest winter weather in leggings, bootlings, and a matchcoat.

Historians differ as to when the Powhatan chiefdom came into existence. Most scholars think that about 1570 Wahunsenacawh inherited about five or six tribes clustered together at the confluence of the James and Appomattox Rivers. During the next several decades he increased the size of the chiefdom through conquest and diplomacy. By the time the English arrived in 1607, the chiefdom extended as mentioned above throughout modern Tidewater Virginia. Scholars estimate that Wahunsenacawh ruled thirty to thirty-two peoples, whose languages were dialects of one language family.

Europeans visited the Chesapeake Bay sporadically in the sixteenth century. The Spanish claimed the bay on the basis of their possession of Florida, which they believed stretched to the bay (*Bahia de Santa Maria* being the Spanish name). Powhatans knew much about Europeans when the English arrived, for they not only had had direct experience with the Spanish, but indirect experiences through cultural interchange with native populations in the southeast.

Hernan de Soto's expedition between 1539 and 1542 left a bitter taste in the mouths of southeastern natives, for de Soto and his men treated them abominably. They seized native leaders and held them hostage for food and guides. The slightest resistance from natives meant terrible punishments such as cutting off feet or hands. The Spanish plundered any goods they deemed valuable, like freshwater pearls. Evidence from English sources points out that the Powhatans were initially wary of the English, believing they might be Spanish.

Powhatans also had more direct experience with Spaniards. In 1570 a small expedition of Jesuit priests came to the peninsula to establish a mission somewhere near modern-day Yorktown. They brought with them as a guide a young native who had been kidnapped by an earlier Spanish expedition to the area. Named Don Luis de Velasco in Spain, the young man promised to provide shelter and food for the missionaries, but quickly returned to his native people on the peninsula. A few days later he led a war party against the missionaries, killing all but a young acolyte. In 1572 Spanish retaliation for this assault resulted in the shelling and destruction of a Powhatan village. To the Powhatans, Spanish response was disproportionate to the original offense. Although revenge was a general cause for war for the Powhatans, they usually fought only small-scale skirmishes and battles.

The Powhatan also had some experience with English approaches to relations with native peoples, for the English attempted settlements on Roanoke Island in modern-day North Carolina. Roanoke, located inside the barrier islands known as the Outer Banks, was the scene of two failed attempts at settlement in the mid-1580s. Sir Walter Ralegh sponsored the expeditions from monies he made seizing and exploiting large landed estates during the English wars on Ireland in the 1560s and 1570s. Ralegh called the region Virginia in honor of Queen Elizabeth I, the Virgin Queen, who reigned 1558–1603. Ralegh, who never came to Virginia, tried to establish first a military/trading base (1585–1586) and second a permanent, agricultural colony (1587). An English military expedition from the first colony made its way overland to the southern shore of the Chesapeake during the 1585–1586 attempt. Evidence indicates that some Lost Colony members (the 1587 attempt) came to the southern end of the bay and settled there sometime in the late 1580s or early 1590s. Each of these settlement attempts brought strained relations between the English and their native hosts, especially the 1585–1586 one.

In addition to Roanoke settlement attempts, English sailing expeditions stopped along the Atlantic coast of Virginia in the decades between the 1587 Roanoke attempt and the 1607 Jamestown settlement. By the time the English did begin permanent settlement at Jamestown, the Powhatans had much contact with them.

England's 1607 Virginia settlement was the product of private investment encouraged by England's ruler King James I (1603–1625). British merchants financed most seventeenth-century English settlements throughout the world. Using an investment format called the joint-stock company, English entrepreneurs interested in trade and evangelization activities solicited monies from investors. The Virginia Company, chartered in 1606 by James I, provided the capital, supplies, leadership, and manpower to begin and sustain the small settlement at Jamestown. The Virginia Company had two branches, one in London and the other in Plymouth. The Plymouth branch received a charter for the northern reaches of the company's grant from James I. The London branch obtained its charter for the grant's southerly reaches.

In December 1606 three ships, the *Susan Constant*, the *Godspeed*, and the *Discovery* left London for Virginia. Admiral Christopher Newport commanded the expedition. About 105 men and boys formed the first colony. The company had instructed that a president and council govern the colony on site and that proved to be divisive and factionalizing when the colony began. When the expedition arrived in late April 1607 at the mouth of the Chesapeake Bay, exploratory parties located a site for settlement. About forty miles upriver from the mouth of the James, the site's major attraction was that oceangoing ships of the day could tie up almost at the shore since the water at Jamestown Island was so deep. A swampy, marshy region, the site had mosquitoes and other insect pests, little readily available freshwater, and, aside from red cedar, few easily exploited resources colonists could send to England for the company to sell. Company investors expected to make money off the capital they had put in. Those who went on the early expeditions were either "adventurers of purse or person," meaning they either had bought at least one share of company stock (purse) or sold their labor (person) to the company for seven years. In the first expedition the ratio was about 50–50, not good when adventurers of purse were not generally required to work on behalf of the company. It was left to the company's laborers to perform the tasks of fort construction, house building, and crop planting. The company, however, instructed the colonials to secure a one-year's supply of food from the "naturals," the natives of the area. The Indians generally balked at such treatment, especially when the settlers' leadership told them they would be there only a few weeks.

The Jamestown settlement had many purposes, as set out by the company's "instructions" sent with the first group. Among those instructions the company's managers included directions to find gold or other immediately exploitable commodities, establish trade with local natives, secure the region from Spanish intrusion (England's principal enemy at the time), find a convenient route to the South Sea (Pacific Ocean) so that England could trade directly with China and Japan, and seek any survivors of the 1587 Roanoke settlement (the Lost Colony). In effect, the early settlement at Jamestown was a combination military outpost and trading station, called a "factory" at that time. During Jamestown's early years settlers found sassafras and red cedar as exploitable commodities, experimented with making glass, mapped and charted the Chesapeake Bay and its tributary rivers, and sought a way to the South Sea. Very little succeeded.

Settlement leaders included Council President Edward-Maria Wingfield and councilors Bartholomew Gosnold, John Ratcliffe, John Smith, John Martin,

George Kendall, and Reverend Robert Hunt. This system proved fractious and unsettling, for personality clashes among the councilors often led to open disputes within the settlement generally as individual councilors sought to build their own factions among the other settlers. Powhatan natives willingly supplied hospitality and taught Europeans how to grow their own food, but they needed their own supplies for winter and early spring use. There was also another serious problem affecting food supply.

Recent climatological investigations show that a prolonged drought, one of the worst in the last 800 years, began in eastern Virginia when the English arrived. The drought was part of a longer-term series of climate shifts generally called the Little Ice Age, during which the northern hemisphere cooled considerably between 1300 and 1600. From 1600 until about 1850 a much cooler climate prevailed, with the lowest temperatures occurring during the 1690s. This climate change had profound effects on human health and agriculture the world over, causing or abetting droughts, plagues, rainfall saturation, and major population migrations. In early seventeenth-century Virginia the onset of the Little Ice Age meant drought conditions that severely constrained native production of food. It also meant a higher than normal salt concentration in the rivers due to lower rainfall amounts.

Conflicts between local Powhatan peoples and the English over food soon became complicated with contests for land. The English believed Indians needed much less land than they claimed and the English, like all European Christians of the time, believed God in *Genesis* had given Christians sole dominion over the lands of the earth. All others simply inhabited those lands until Christians could dispossess them. The English in Virginia believed Indians possessed only a "right in the soil" that the English might easily extinguish through purchase or, if that did not work, through war. Early food confrontations soon coupled with land conflicts to produce a war that lasted from 1609 until 1614 and ended only when the English, with the cooperation of the Potomac Indians' weroance, kidnapped Powhatan's favorite daughter Pocahontas and ransomed her for peace. John Rolfe, the Englishman responsible for successfully introducing tobacco as a cash commodity crop in Virginia agriculture, fell in love with Pocahontas during her captivity and offered to marry her. When her father accepted the proposal and marriage occurred, the event marked the conclusion of the peace treaty between the two peoples.

During the next few years the English expanded their lands along the James River, displacing native peoples on both sides of the river from their homelands. They also began some settlements on the Eastern Shore, but little occupation of the interior of the peninsula or the York River valley happened until the 1620s. In that decade renewed warfare occurred, for many of the same reasons as the first one. English demand for native lands, English refusal to return unused lands to the "common pot," pressures for food, and, especially after 1618, increased pressure on natives to surrender their traditional culture prompted the outbreak of war in 1622. The war lasted for ten years and was the impetus to begin active settlement at Middle Plantation, or as it was renamed in 1699, Williamsburg.

Chapter Two

WILLIAMSBURG BEFORE IT WAS WILLIAMSBURG: MIDDLE PLANTATION IN THE SEVENTEENTH CENTURY

In the seventeenth century Anglo-Virginia colonists called the site that became Williamsburg Middle Plantation. No evidence, either documentary or archaeological, survives indicating native habitation of the site itself. At least three peoples of the Powhatan chiefdom, the Pasbehays, Kiskiacks, and Kecoughtans, lived near the site. The Pasbehays lived along the James River a few miles upriver from where the English intruded in 1607. The Pasbehays had moved to the upriver site from the site of Jamestown just a few years before, an illustration of the long fallow agriculture Powhatans practiced at the time of contact. The Kiskiacks lived across the peninsula near what is now Yorktown. The Kecoughtans lived at the peninsula's end. They farmed several hundred acres, probably to create a storehouse for peninsula natives and the Powhatan Chieftainship generally. As mentioned in chapter one, the Powhatans preferred living along rivers or streams, so they did not often build a village in the interior. Williamsburg's site, located on the ridge separating the James and York Rivers, does not appear to have had native dwellers. Although people have found thousands of projectile points in Williamsburg, no evidence of long-term occupation has yet been discovered within the town's geographic boundaries. Finding so many projectile points suggests that natives used the area for hunting rather than dwelling.

Recently, however, an archaeological team discovered a habitation just outside the city's limits dating to between 1,000 and 2,000 years ago. It has two fire hearths, one inside and the other outside the building. The structure is large enough to have been a dwelling for several people. The team has yet to find any other buildings or indications that the site might have been a village, but searching continues.

Settlement at the site that became Middle Plantation began as a consequence of a war that broke out between Anglo-Virginians and the Powhatans in 1622. Since the English intruded into Virginia in 1607, they sought a profit-making commodity that the London Company, the colony's parent, could sell in England and on the continent. Company workers tried several experiments, from glassmaking, wine grape growing, to silkworm raising for instance, but nothing worked until John Rolfe experimented with tobacco. When Rolfe, who married Pocahontas on April 5, 1614, succeeded in 1615 in producing a useable form of tobacco, the Virginia Company finally found its profit making commodity.

Rolfe adapted a mild West Indian form of tobacco to Virginia's light sandy soils. Tobacco is a very heavy feeder, leaching much fertility from soils, especially relatively weak ones like Tidewater Virginia's, and quickly exhausts land. As tobacco growing expanded, the company began sending much larger contingents of workers and settlers in 1618 and after. The combination of demand for new lands the workers needed and replacement lands for those already wearing out from tobacco, placed great pressure on peninsula natives to surrender portions of their traditional hunting lands. In addition, English missionaries increased efforts to convert Powhatans to Christianity. Anglo-Virginians misread Powhatan curiosity about Christianity, believing they were hungry for conversion. After 1618, the company stepped up efforts to convert natives, even laying plans for the construction of an Indian college near modern-day Richmond where conversion might be carried out under missionary aegis.

Wahunsenacawh died in 1617, leaving two brothers, Opitacham and Opechancanough, as claimants to his authority. Opitacham, the next older after Wahunsenacawh, inherited the title of Powhatan. Many think that Opitacham died soon thereafter, but others think he survived for several years as titular leader of the chiefdom. However leadership passed, and Opechancanough seems to have wielded the actual power of the chiefdom. Professing his friendship and affection for the Anglo-Virginians, Opechancanough secretly laid plans for an all-out assault on the English. The murder of one of his favorites, Nemattanow (Jack-of-the-Feather), prompted his execution of the plan for the secret attack. It took place on March 22, 1622, and resulted in the loss of about one-fifth of the Anglo-Virginian population. With about 1,250 survivors, English Virginia could have either succumbed or begun the long, horrendous war that lasted about ten years. The intruders chose war and used tactics that made even the English at home squeamish.

By 1632 the natives could no longer hold out and so made peace. The construction of Middle Plantation was part of the defense posture the English erected on the peninsula. The idea for Middle Plantation arose from investigations made by a Royal Commission sent to Virginia after the 1622 surprise attack. Asked for ideas about protection from such future attacks, the colonials replied that a palisade, much like those the English constructed in Ireland in the late sixteenth century during the English invasion of Ireland, should be constructed across the peninsula. Anchoring the palisade in the middle would be a settlement or plantation. Both an agricultural and military outpost, Middle Plantation would serve as primary guard station along the palisade. Although Samuel Mathews of Denbigh and William Claiborne of

Williamsburg

Kecoughtan offered in 1626 to construct the palisade for £1,000 and maintain it for £100 per year, the Assembly, created as an advisory board to the governor in 1619, evidently did not take them up on the offer. Between 1630 and 1633, however, Anglo-Virginians did build the palisade, using the offer of free land as an incentive. Some of the largest land patents taken out along it included Dr. John Pott's 1,200 acres in July 1632. Within a few years, the palisade and the settlement named Middle Plantation coexisted along the line stretching from the head of Archers Hope Creek (known now as College Creek) to Queen's Creek, and some settlements existed on the south side of the York River near the north end of the palisade. At the same time, to make local government available the colonial government, royal since 1624, created Virginia's first eight counties: James City, Elizabeth City, York, Isle of Wight, Surry, Henrico, Charles City, and Northampton.

Created to keep natives out of the eastern end of the lower peninsula and to use as a staging base for assaults on the natives, the palisade soon fell into neglect after the war ended, although Middle Plantation remained a viable settlement. Settlers soon noticed that mosquitoes infested the area less than at Jamestown, a place notorious for its swamps and marshes in which the pests bred. Built along the ridge of the peninsula and sufficiently high enough that water drained into the York from the north side of the ridge and the James from the south side, the ridge provided some respite from the unhealthy conditions of Jamestown itself. Also, the ridge served as the most convenient roadway down the peninsula because the creeks and streams that fed into the two main rivers blocked easy road construction close to the river shores.

Others who took up lands included Richard Popeley, who patented 1,250 acres just west of the palisade. The colonial government appointed him commanding officer of Middle Plantation. Born in Wooley parish, Yorkshire in 1598, Popeley came to Virginia in 1620 and lived in Elizabeth City borough/county until he moved to Middle Plantation to take up his duties in the late 1630s. Like so many other early settlers, Popeley died in 1643 and left no heirs. Although opportunity existed for those with ties of blood or business in England in the years after Virginia became royal, many of those who took advantage of such opportunities had no heirs. Their estates, landed and otherwise, often remained unclaimed in the colony for decades. Such lands that remained unclaimed were one other irritant that bred native discontent as they saw lands they had once inhabited and used untouchable because the English declared the lands private property, a concept natives found difficult to understand.

By the mid-1640s, when another war with Native Americans occurred, the palisade had so deteriorated that the Assembly ordered Captain Robert Higginson to rebuild and refortify it, again using Middle Plantation as the center of the defense work. In the meantime, other English immigrants took up lands in and around the settlement. John Clerke, nephew of Sir John Clerke, Kent County, England, bought 850 acres from Richard Popeley in the early 1640s. Like Popeley, Clerke died without heirs in 1646. Edward and George Wyatt, sons of Reverend Hawte Wyatt, an early minister at Jamestown, and nephews of Sir Francis Wyatt, an early governor of the colony, acquired lands on the site in the settlement. Stephen Hamlin and George Lake acquired 400 and 250 acres of land respectively adjoining Popeley's lands. Henry Tyler, an ancestor of John Tyler (the U.S. President) and Lyon Gardiner Tyler (a president of William and Mary), obtained 254 acres of land that would eventually become William and Mary College.

Richard Kempe, the colony's secretary in the 1640s, obtained the largest amounts of land near Middle Plantation, some 4,332 acres on both sides of Archer's Hope Creek. A plat in the Virginia Historical Society's archives shows the lands along with a horse path running through it; the path eventually became Duke of Gloucester Street. About 1660 Kempe's lands passed to Thomas Ludwell, his successor as the colony's secretary. In the late 1890s and early 1900s, archaeological investigations found old tiles and bricks marking the site of the habitation of the two secretaries.

After the English Restoration in 1660, other figures began taking lands in the settlement. Otho Thorpe, a relative of George Thorpe killed in the 1622 attack, had a large house in Middle Plantation, one in which the Assembly met in the 1680s and in which Nathaniel Bacon Jr. had urged his followers in 1676 to revolt against English authority. Bacon, attempting to expel Governor Sir William Berkeley from the colony, used Thorpe's house in early August to encourage his followers to resist English attempts at restoring Berkeley's authority. He offered his followers at the house an oath proclaiming him the rightful ruler of Virginia. Berkeley, once his forces had suppressed the rebels, used Thorpe's house for some trials and executions of the rebels, the most notable being William Drummond in early January 1677.

English troops assigned to suppress the rebellion quartered in Middle Plantation after their arrival in early spring 1677. Although Berkeley and his followers had largely crushed the rebels, the troops remained in Virginia for the next several years, living at the settlement. In 1677 the Assembly set aside 200 acres in Middle Plantation for the troops to plant and raise food for themselves while stationed in the colony. The troops remained in the colony for several years after the rebellion to aid suppressing additional unrest that cropped up.

Since Anglo-American societies had no police forces in the seventeenth century, the colonists built a public magazine in Middle Plantation to store powder, ammunition, and arms for suppressing unrest and uprisings. Where the magazine stood is unknown. While military activity of this sort went on in 1677, the leader of the three-man royal commission assigned to investigate Bacon's Rebellion, Sir Herbert Jeffreys, negotiated a treaty at Middle Plantation with Virginia Indians that made them tributary forever to the Virginia government. The Middle Plantation treaty stipulated that native leaders would annually present a deer to the colony's governor as a token of their tribute to the colony. The treaty originally provided that such presentation be made "at the going away of the geese" yearly, meaning in early spring. Eventually, however, the presentation moved to just before Thanksgiving and today Virginia's Native American leaders present the tribute to the governor annually on the steps of the executive mansion a few days before Thanksgiving.

Bacon and his followers had occupied the traditional capital, Jamestown, in August and September 1676, but when they withdrew, they burned it. While the town underwent reconstruction after the rebellion ended, the Assembly met several times at Middle Plantation, usually at Otho Thorpe's house in the settlement. In 1678 York County residents petitioned the Assembly to move the capital to Middle Plantation, asserting as one reason for their request its proximity to the rest of the colony's population. During the latter half of the seventeenth century, Virginia's colonial population shifted from the James River valley to river valleys to the north—the York, Rappahannock, and Potomac. The York residents' petition recognized that shift. They also wanted the colonial capital closer to their own residences and farms. Finally, they seemed to understand the greater healthfulness of the settlement. But the colony's leaders rejected the petition at the time.

Several important figures in seventeenth-century Virginia's developing society lived at Middle Plantation during and after Bacon's Rebellion. Daniel Parke, an ancestor of Daniel Parke Custis, Martha Washington's first husband, died in March 1679 at his home in Middle Plantation. He was buried inside Bruton Parish Church. Parke migrated from England and acquired significant lands during his life in Virginia. Another resident, James Bray, sat on the colonial council until his death in 1691. John Page, another councilor, also died in Middle Plantation in 1692. The council combined three important governmental functions: an advisory board to the colony's governor, the upper house of the Virginia colonial legislature, and, with the governor, the colony's highest appellate court. Council members living in Middle Plantation indicate a population shift away from Jamestown where earlier in the century most councilors had lived.

Middle Plantation also became the home of two institutions that became major centers of society and power in eighteenth-century Williamsburg, Bruton Parish Church and The College of William and Mary. Founded in the latter half of the seventeenth century, these two institutions played strong roles in the shift of the capital from Jamestown to Williamsburg in 1699.

Bruton Parish Church resulted from the merger of two Middle Plantation parishes in the mid-seventeenth century. The parishes, created in the first half of the century, represented the Anglican faith. The Church of England was the official state church of colonial Virginia, as it was of England itself. The Assembly created the two parishes, Middle Plantation and Harrop, in 1633 and 1644 respectively, only to unite the two into Middletown Parish in 1648. In 1654 the Assembly created Marston Parish and united it with Middletown to make Bruton Parish in 1674. The name most likely derived from Bruton, Somerset County, England, the town from which Sir Thomas Ludwell, the colony's secretary, migrated.

A church existed at least as early as 1665 in Middle Plantation; it was probably a frame building (not brick) and not located on the site where the current Bruton Parish church sits. By 1670 it had come to be called the Old Church, but in 1674 the newly-created Bruton Parish vestry directed that a brick church be constructed on a site given the parish by John Page. The church's construction, however, took nine years, due in part to Bacon's Rebellion and its aftermath. Reverend Rowland Jones, the first Anglican minister to preside over the finished church, conducted the first service on November 29, 1683. He formally dedicated the new church on January 6, 1684.

A few details exist about this new parish church. For instance, women had to sit on the left side of the church, while men sat on its north, or right, side. Once William and Mary College began its operations, the vestry set aside a gallery for students. The gallery's door had a lock and key, kept in the possession of the sexton. He perhaps locked the students in the gallery during service so that they might not slip out. Once the colonial capital moved to Williamsburg in 1699, Bruton Parish Church became the leading church in the colony. The center of worship for the colonial governor and many of his councilors, it assumed great symbolic importance in the eighteenth century. The church sat on what became Duke of Gloucester Street about one third of the way between the College and Capitol building. It had the Governor's Palace just to its east. As the eighteeenth century progressed, the church became the court church of the colonial capital.

The other important institution, The College of William and Mary, began as a consequence of the church and its importance in Middle Plantation. Chartered in 1693, the college is located at the junction of Richmond and Jamestown Roads, where they meet Duke of Gloucester Street. At the time of William and Mary's founding, Duke of Gloucester Street was a horsepath, Richmond Road was Old Stage Road (later the King's Highway), and Jamestown Road was already known by that name.

Williamsburg

The creation of the college arose from general concern in official English circles about the status of the Anglican Church in the colonies. English officials wondered how they might foster its growth. Just before Bacon's Rebellion, for instance, a plan was developed to make Jamestown an episcopal center by constructing a cathedral in the town. Although all official procedures seem to have been completed by 1674, the crown never issued the formal proclamation. In the meantime, the bishop of London had acted as the head of the colonial church. He only had power, however, to license ministers to preach in the colonies.

In 1675, Charles II named Henry Compton the Bishop of London and he began trying to rectify clerical abuses in the colonies. Abuses included drinking on the job, failure to conduct services at appropriate times, and trying to obtain two or more parishes in order to enhance ministerial salaries. Compton decided to create commissaries for each colony, clerical positions that would report to him from the colonies, giving him fresh perspectives and insights on church business. He appointed James Blair as his commissary for Virginia. Reverend Blair, already in the colony at a parish in Henrico County, took up his duties as commissary in June 1690. He promptly summoned the Virginia clergy to a convention to discuss two issues. The first concerned developing and carrying out a plan for a more convenient execution of ecclesiastical discipline in the colony. The second issue concerned the foundation of a seminary in the colony to train new ministers. Blair did not like Jamestown; he preferred Middle Plantation and he took every opportunity to transfer power and authority to that settlement. As commissary he had power to do all that a Bishop of the Church of England could except ordain priests and confirm individuals. His plan for a college meant that even those young men who chose to get an education at the college would have to go to England for ordination.

The plan Blair developed called for the creation of an Indian school as well as the college. The college, however, would educate those young men not interested in the ministerial profession. So it would serve three purposes: train future ministers for the colony, educate young Native-American males in how to become Christians, and finish the higher education of young men in the colony. Blair secured the charter for the college in 1693 and named it in honor of the reigning monarchs, William and Mary. The name also commemorates the Glorious Revolution in which the English ejected James II (Stuart) and his family from the English throne. Parliament then called William and Mary (she was the older Protestant daughter of James by his first wife) to the throne. The Glorious Revolution completed a dramatic change in English government that transformed it into a constitutional monarchy with the reign of William and Mary.

The college's original colors were orange and white (the official colors of the House of Orange, William's Dutch household), again commemorating the Protestant nature of the Glorious Revolution. Blair received a total of £1,985 14s 10d in the charter toward the expenses of foundation. The money was to come from the Colony's annual quitrents. In addition, the college received a 1d-per-pound duty on all tobacco exported from the Chesapeake to cover annual expenses. The college consisted initially of a chancellor, a president or rector, six professors, and a board of eighteen visitors to run the institution. The college was to pay annually as tribute for the charter two copies of Latin verse written by students and faculty during the year. The college delivered these verses to the governor every November 5, the anniversary of the famous Gunpowder Plot. Blair also raised money for the college. In 1693, as the charter was being readied, the Virginia government captured three pirates who had been raiding in the James River. The three, Edward Davis, Lionell Delawayfer, and Jonathan Hinson, agreed to give Blair £300 of the silver they stole in return for their freedom. The £300 went into the coffers for construction of the csollege.

By 1698 Middle Plantation had become an established settlement, though not in the shape and form that Williamsburg would eventually take. It had two institutions that would become characteristic of the future colonial capital, Bruton Parish Church and The College of William and Mary. By that time, Jamestown had been the capital of the colony since 1607. That early settlement had burned on several occasions and in October 1698 the statehouse in Jamestown burned for the fourth time during the century. Colonial officials suspected Arthur Jarvis of setting the fire, but no evidence surfaced to prove his alleged arson. The Assembly once again debated moving the capital; this time it determined to do so. Tradition has it that very moving pleas by students of the new college clinched the decision. The students asked that the capital be moved from Jamestown to Middle Plantation. In 1699 the Assembly accepted the appeals and made the decision, and Middle Plantation became Williamsburg.

Chapter Three

WILLIAMSBURG BECOMES WILLIAMSBURG: THE EIGHTEENTH CENTURY, 1699–1754

In May and June 1699, newly-appointed Lieutenant-Governor Francis Nicholson and the Virginia Assembly drafted and passed legislation that moved the colonial capital from Jamestown to Middle Plantation and renamed the site Williamsburg in honor of English King William III. William, the royal consort of Mary Stuart, the Protestant elder daughter of James II's first marriage, ascended the English throne on the death of his wife in 1698. The English Parliament called William III and Mary II to the throne in 1689 during the Glorious Revolution, a bloodless coup that overthrew James II. Mary and her husband, the Dutch Republic's chief executive, ruled England as constitutional monarchs, the first such monarchs in English history.

Nicholson had already served as Virginia governor in his career, during the early 1690s. Then the imperial government moved him to Annapolis, the new capital of Maryland, where he served as governor until re-appointment to Virginia in 1698. As governor of both Chesapeake Bay colonies, he took active part in designing the capital towns of each colony. During his stint in Maryland, he created the town plan and several basic building designs for Annapolis. That experience served him well as he designed Williamsburg.

Town planning and design were more the rule than the exception in the early English Empire. Men like Nicholson, General James Oglethorpe, and William Penn and their advisers and assistants participated in surveying, designing, laying out, and supervising construction of towns like Annapolis, Williamsburg, Savannah, and Philadelphia, according to architectural and town planning historian John W. Reps. Although Nicholson may have conceived the basic outline and design, the layout and construction of Williamsburg occupied many people in the early eighteenth century. If Nicholson was responsible for the basic town design and beginning construction of important public buildings during his second tenure as governor, Alexander Spotswood (governed 1710–1722) was responsible for completing the basic public construction of the city. Nicholson laid out the town, oversaw construction of the capitol building, and sought monies for building other edifices. Spotswood completed the capitol, rebuilt the college after a disastrous fire in 1705, completed the "Governor's Palace" begun under Governor Edward Nott (1705–1709), built the powder magazine, rebuilt Bruton Parish Church, and laid out and began Market Square. All this is getting ahead of the story, however.

When Nicholson proposed that the capital be moved to Middle Plantation, several William and Mary College students participated in the proposal for such relocation. In May 1699, five students delivered speeches to the Assembly arguing for the move. Good markets, convenience of good company and conversation, a healthier site than Jamestown (heavily infested with malaria-bearing mosquitoes), excellent access to creeks and streams feeding into the James and York Rivers, and safety from Native-American attacks (because it was inland from the rivers) were just parts of the rationale the college students introduced in what was probably a very carefully orchestrated (by Nicholson and Commissary Blair) series of presentations. Advantages included a union of town and gown (at least 100 people resided annually at the college); the need for tradesmen, artisans, and craftsmen to construct the town, its public buildings, and college together; and the union of intellect, religion, and politics symbolized by the college, church, and capitol buildings. The Assembly gave its approval and included provision for the location of two ports, to be sited near the heads of two creeks that came within a mile of the new city respectively (see Theodorick Bland's survey of the proposed city boundaries).

At the time, Middle Plantation, on the narrowest portion of the peninsula, consisted of Bruton Parish Church, the college and associated grammar school, two mills, a smithy, a few stores, and some houses. Joined by a winding path usually called a horse path, the setting was less a village than a community. The Assembly appropriated over 283 acres (including provisions for the two ports), with the city itself receiving 220 of those acres.

Governor Nicholson used Middle Plantation's topography as the basis for designing the town. A ridge, serving as a watershed for creeks into the James and York Rivers, provided the route for what became the central avenue of the new city—Duke of Gloucester Street (named for Queen Anne's eldest son and heir apparent to the English throne; he died before his mother, however). At each end of the street and anchoring it with vistas were to be the college and capitol.

Legislation approving the capitol's construction passed the Assembly the same time that the bill passed creating the town itself (June 1699). The capitol was designed as an H with each wing the home of one of the two houses of the colonial Assembly. The House of Burgesses, the elected body representing the colony's eligible voters (property-owning, white, adult males), was housed on one side. The council and general court, consisting of the twelve councilors advising the governor, and the governor himself occupied the other wing. The portico joining the two wings became the central meeting place for working out legislation contested between the two houses.

Hugh Jones, first professor of mathematics at the college, arrived in Williamsburg in the late 1710s. He remained on William and Mary's faculty for only a few years, removing to Maryland in the 1720s where he spent the rest of his life. He commented in his *Present State of Virginia* that:

> there are two fine Publick Buildings in this Country, which are the most Magnificent of any in America: One of which is the College before spoken of, and the other the Capitol or State-House, as it was formerly call'd: That is, the House for Convention of the General Assembly, for the Setting of the General Court, for the Meeting of the Council, and for keeping of their several Offices.

Jones also told his readers that private houses:

> are of late very much improved; several Gentlemen there, having built themselves large Brick Houses of many Rooms on a Floor, and several Stories high, as also some Stone-Houses: but they don't covet to make them lofty, having extent enough of Ground to build upon; and now and then they are visited by high Winds, which wou'd incommode a towring Fabrick.

Such private houses were not confined to the country or outskirts of Williamsburg, for they began to show up in town while Jones taught at William and Mary.

Construction began on the capitol early in the eighteenth century and continued through the early decades. In the meantime, wary Virginians balked at buying town lots. The 1698 enabling legislation provided that half-acre lots be sold at auction. The Assembly created a group of twelve trustees who were to rate the lands surveyed by Bland and pay from the proceeds of land sales in the town the original landowners, men such as John Page and Henry Tyler. Not until about 1720 did Virginians feel secure enough about the new city to purchase land in it. Everyone who bought a lot had by law to build a house on it within two years. Each building was to be set back six feet from the street line, which for Duke of Gloucester was ninety-nine feet wide. With some leveling by 1730 of the streambeds and rivulets that crossed Duke of Gloucester, that street was roughly three-fourths of a mile long, bounded at each end by the capitol and college, and generally regarded as a very attractive place on which to walk and shop.

Nicholson and his immediate successors, Edward Nott and Alexander Spotswood, further developed the design of the city. According to Reps, Nicholson made Bruton

Parish Church the center of one large rectangle, projected to be the residential center of the town. From the church's eastern boundary northward was the site set aside for construction of the governor's house, ultimately to be called the Governor's Palace (originally a derogatory reference generated by over-large expenditures for its building but later adopted as the familiar name for it). The trustees acquired more lands to the north of the palace in order to create gardens and walks on English gardening principles. Many other gardens and walks in the rapidly building city depended on French gardening ideas and designs.

As Nott and Spotswood struggled for funds and supplies to construct the palace, Spotswood oversaw the building of the octagonal-shaped powder magazine. Constructed to house military stores, Spotswood designed the building with extra-thick walls and placed an exterior wall several feet outside as precaution against explosions. In the meantime, the college (called the Wren Building) burned in 1705 and required several years to rebuild, with modifications to the original design.   The major public buildings (the capitol, Governor's Palace, public gaol (jail), powder magazine, Bruton Parish Church, and the college) anchored the plan and design of the city, providing vistas and views from many different angles for citizens and visitors alike.

According to Reps, Nicholson's original plan laid out the city in two large rectangles, the smaller one at the eastern end for public purposes and the larger one at the western end for residences and more private purposes. Between the capitol near the eastern boundary of the city to Market Square about halfway to the college rested the public area. Merchants, artisans, craftsmen, and innkeepers bought lots and built their stores and craft shops in that area. By 1750, a printshop (begun in 1728 by William Parks, who launched the *Virginia Gazette* in 1736), a gunsmith, blacksmith, cabinetmaker, wig and peruke maker, mantua maker, cooper, carriage maker, wheelwright, and several silversmiths and jewelers flourished along or near Duke of Gloucester Street. Inns, ordinaries, and taverns such as Raleigh Tavern, Kings' Arms, Christiana Campbell's, Chownings', and Market Square Tavern also sprang up. Located generally in the "public" area of the city, these public houses provided more than just refreshment and lodging. Games, conversation, politics, economic exchange, and socializing during the workday were all part of the milieu the taverns and inns gave the city.

Nicholson's original design, and modifications by subsequent governors, built in green spaces where public activities such as marketing took place. These included Market Square, located across Duke of Gloucester Street from the powder magazine, and the Palace Green. Market Square held the semi-weekly farmers' markets

(Wednesdays and Saturdays) during which residents, farmers, and planters from outside town came together to exchange produce, meat (live and butchered), and many other supplies necessary to the townspeople. Market Square also hosted semi-annual fairs (St. George's Day, April 23, and December 12) during which, along with the exchange of foods and manufactured goods, entertainments such as games, minstrels, street shows, and auctions occupied the townspeople and out-of-town visitors.

"Publick Times" also provided opportunities for socializing as the town's population swelled from its usual 1,500–2,000 to 6,000–10,000 (depending on the occasion). "Publick Times" meant the meetings of the General Court (governor and council as the colony's supreme court), Courts of Oyer and Terminer (the same people, but meeting as special court for trials of slaves), and Assembly (governor, councilors, and burgesses). The officials brought their personal slaves, sometimes their families or portions thereof, and friends to "Publick Times." Citizens who had business with the courts or Assemblies further swelled the town's population. Taverns, inns, and ordinaries filled to capacity and often over capacity during the sessions. Visitors often had to find lodging with friends or acquaintances in town or just outside town.

Just to the east of the capitol was a large, open area known today as the Exchange. There ship captains walked with tobacco planters, merchants, factors, and other members of the colony's complex economic web to discuss prices and markets for tobacco and other Virginia products sold in imperial or international trade. Each year a large fleet of merchant ships arrived in the Chesapeake to engage in the tobacco trade. By 1750, tens of millions of pounds of tobacco left the bay for sale in English, colonial, and continental markets. Tobacco was one of the more lucrative agricultural enterprises of the English Empire. Although designed as a political and cultural capital, Williamsburg also served an economic purpose as one of the important centers of tobacco trade in the colony.

As Virginia's prosperity expanded during the second quarter of the eighteenth century, house lot owners in Williamsburg began constructing or reconstructing their homes. Artisan or craftsman homeowners generally combined their shop and home, not uncommon in the pre-industrial world when most households were integral parts of the economy. James Geddy, a master silversmith, is an example of such a craftsman. His family, slaves, apprentices, journeymen, and maids all lived in the household in the mid-eighteenth century while pursuing economic elements of a silversmith's life in town.

Major tobacco planters, especially if they served as members of the colony's council, had town homes to which they came to during "Publick Times," or for what passed in the eighteenth century as a vacation. One of the early residents of the city, Daniel Parke II, served in Parliament in the eighteenth century. He had fought in Marlborough's army in the War of the Spanish Succession (1701–1713) at the battle of Blenheim particularly, the news of which he carried to Queen Anne (1702–1714). Other prominent Virginians included Robert Carter Nicholas, the Paradise family, and the Ludwells, all of whom had homes in town that were generally much more refined than those of craftsmen or artisans. Other homeowners lived and worked in Williamsburg, not as tobacco planters, artisans, or craftsmen, but as intellectuals. George Wythe took up residence along the Palace Green (as did Robert Carter Nicholas) to be near the seat of power (the governor's mansion in the colonial era) and to be close to William and Mary, at which he taught and tutored students in the law.

As Thad W. Tate notes in his *The Negro in Eighteenth-Century Williamsburg*, fully one-half the city's population, however, took no part in property ownership, did not share in government, and had nothing to do with education, but performed most of the manual labor in the city. These, of course, were the slaves of Williamsburg. Of the approximately 1,500 permanent residents of the city, about 50 percent were African-American slaves. Imported directly from Africa in the early eighteenth century, by 1750 native-born slave children (creoles) slowed the need for fresh imports. By the time of the Revolution in 1775, native-born slaves (usually born in the city itself) comprised the majority of slave sales in town. Average numbers per household in town stood at eight to ten, most being domestic service-cooks (primary importance), butlers and valets, maids, and laundresses. Slave draymen and cartmen worked hauling goods to and from the city's two ports, Queen Mary and Princess Anne. Slaves did most of the heavy labor at those ports, loading tobacco and other exports, and unloading furniture, cartons of dishes, clothing, and other domestic products for the town's households. Slaves did much of the physical labor in construction of the city, public and private buildings alike.

The market values of town slaves rose generally in the eighteenth century, until just before the Revolution; masters advertising slaves for sale asked about £45–50 for a skilled adult slave or £35–40 for a skilled female slave. However, most sales, when completed, registered a sale price of about three quarters the requested sum.

Virginia's Assembly legalized slavery in the early 1660s; it remained legal until the ratification of the 13th Amendment to the United States Constitution in 1865. In 1705, the Assembly codified all earlier slave legislation into the first Slave Code in British colonial North America. The code classified slaves as chattel (moveable) property, but also made them liable for behavior normally defined as criminal in Anglo-American society. Slaves were tried for arson, murder, stealing, and all the other crimes for which any white might be tried. Punishments, however, were more rigorous, usually requiring some form of whipping, branding, or execution. Slaves who ran off could be killed on sight and their owners rewarded from the colony's treasury at whatever market value was attached to the slave before death. Masters or overseers could kill slaves "in the act of correction" (usually whipping) without fear of punishment in colonial and antebellum Virginia. Slaves could not testify in court, for or against whites or other African Americans.

Slaves did most of the physical labor in Williamsburg; they slept wherever they could find a bed (usually on the floor), received whatever food and clothing they had from their masters' families, and had no freedom to go or do what they wished. Masters who needed to settle a debt in town sold a slave or slaves in order to raise the money to cover it. By the third quarter of the eighteenth century a slave auction block existed in front of the Raleigh Tavern where officials sold slaves almost weekly.

Despite their lot, slaves managed to survive in the city; their lives probably somewhat better than their counterparts in the countryside who spent countless hours growing, tending, and harvesting many different kinds of crops, the most important being tobacco. African Americans resisted slavery by running off, slowing their work pace, intentionally breaking tools, or deliberately misinterpreting their masters' instructions, and occasionally either murdering their master or overseer or committing suicide. No records from Williamsburg itself suggest that any slaves murdered their masters or committed suicide. Slaves did run off, usually to hide with family or friends just outside town (often in one of the two ports) or to find family living on a farm or plantation just outside town. Masters often split up and sold family members, especially if a member was recalcitrant or, on the other hand, a well-trained artisan.

Masters also rented out their slaves for periods of time, often a year. The rent money added to their overall value. Such slaves acquired many skills over their lifetime. Trained as a cook or valet, these servants added to their repertoire, at their master's insistence, skills ancillary to the original. They also might develop entirely new skills unrelated to the original. Most Williamsburg householders who owned slaves (not all did) had just a few, and those few usually developed several specialties.

There was another half of the population—women—who were also important to the successful development of the city. Females, black and white alike, contributed to the city's life in many ways, including economic, cultural, social, and, occasionally, political. If slave women had no legal rights, neither did married white women. The English legal code described a woman as femme covert, that is, her legal personality subsumed in that of her husband unless he died, at which time she became a femme sole, meaning she assumed a legal definition of her own. As femme sole, the woman might enter into contracts, conduct a business, sue and be sued, and direct through a will distribution of her property.

Few women in eighteenth-century Williamsburg entered into femme sole status because societal pressures coerced widows to remarry as soon as possible. Yet several women in the city did eventually come to manage enterprises, such as the *Virginia Gazette* or the milliner's shop. If English law generally barred women from direct participation in the economy, colonial conditions conversely encouraged them to do so. Even a city that became as prosperous as Williamsburg needed all the labor and workers it could get.

Women were responsible for bringing children into the world, and childbirth in those days was much more dangerous than today. Mothers had little responsibility for raising the children, contrary to a later day. Husbands, especially of the wealthy elite, assumed much responsibility for childrearing, particularly education, still largely a male province in those days. Mothers taught daughters skills of housewifery, managed the household, participated in the everyday running of the shop (if married to a craftsman), and may have participated in the management of the household with her husband (if he permitted such a role to his wife).

Women not only directed the domestic chores of the household, they usually participated in its economic functions, especially if it was that of an artisan or craftsman. Presumably most artisans' wives worked in the front shop selling the goods produced in the shop (located usually in the rear). Women also engaged in the town's economic life by taking over their deceased husband's activities, at least until they remarried or sold the enterprise to an aspiring journeyman, wishing to become a master of the same craft.

Women may also have played some role in politics, behind the scenes, as advisers to their husbands. Some men who participated actively in politics, both as voters and office seekers or holders, seem to have solicited the advice of their wives. Women could not vote nor could they hold office, in any colony. But some evidence, such as women's diaries and journals, suggest that women by 1750 wished a more active role in the public life of the colonies, Williamsburg included.

By 1720 the city's major public buildings were finished or under construction. The new college was about completed. The Governor's Palace was almost finished, the capitol had been done for several years, and the magazine was also finished. In 1722, King George I granted Williamsburg a charter making it a city within the context of eighteenth-century English legal life. The charter placed political power in the hands of an appointed mayor, a group of six aldermen, and a common council of twelve citizens to be chosen by the mayor and aldermen. The first mayor, John Holloway, was joined by Archibald Blair, James Bray, John Custis, Thomas Jones, John

Randolph, and William Robertson as the first aldermen. John Clayton served as first recorder. This early city government directed political affairs, although both James City and York County governments overlapped Williamsburg's political functions. The counties' dividing line ran (and still runs) down Duke of Gloucester Street.

In the late 1720s and early 1730s the college began expansion with the addition of the Brafferton and the President's House. Built in roughly the same architecture and facing each other across the courtyard approaching the Wren building from the east, the two buildings added a residence for the college's president and a school for Indian boys to be educated in English culture and religion.

Construction of the Indian school, named the Brafferton building, relied on a legacy to the college made by Robert Boyle in his will. One purpose for creating the college was to acculturate Native-American boys, especially sons of influential and leadership families among Indian peoples still resident in the colony, to Anglo-Virginia ways. As one Native-American chief, however, described it early in the eighteenth century, the boys were fit neither for Indian nor European society. Eventually the Brafferton became a dormitory for college students.

As the college symbolized the colony's early commitment to higher education, Bruton Parish Church represented the colony's commitment to the Church of England. Its proximity to the Governor's Palace, the capitol, and the college made it the principal or leading church, and its services set the tone for the rest of the colony. Built in the form of a Roman cross, the building contained relics from the early Anglican churches at Jamestown, especially a silver church service consisting of three pieces—a chalice, a paten, and an alms plate. In addition, a font in the church was by tradition used at Jamestown's church, again until relocation of the capital to Williamsburg.

The church was a focal point for community life for both Middle Plantation and Williamsburg, more so for the latter with the governor, council, and many burgesses, as well as local leaders attending services at it. A painting imaginatively reconstructing a Sunday at the church shows eighteenth-century planters and their families arriving for services. The painting illustrates the hierarchical organization of eighteenth-century Virginia society, displaying planters' wealth in the coaches and carriages, the slaves as coachmen and footmen, and the absence of "middling sorts," those of the yeoman or artisan groups of Virginia's colonial society. The bell tower at the western end, the brick wall surrounding the church yard, and the absence of other buildings in the scene suggest that the artist portrayed the building in the late seventeenth century, before Williamsburg's construction began.

In the colonial era, bells were generally associated with churches and the Bruton Parish church bells were no exception. One installed in 1761 was a gift of James

Tarpley, a prominent citizen of Williamsburg. Tradition has it that Queen Anne, passing through London on a royal occasion, stopped at a foundry casting a church bell. Told the bell was destined for a church in one of Her Majesty's colonies (Virginia), she impulsively took off much of her silver jewelry and threw it into the molten metal to become part of the bell. Allegedly, that bell became the second bell at Bruton Parish Church and her silver supposedly accounted for the bell's silvery tone.

Stories abound about the buildings and houses of eighteenth-century Williamsburg. One such account chronicles the tale of a small, one-story white cottage in which, at the time of the Revolution, lived an older woman by herself. Known in town for her piety, in the words of Mary L. Foster in *Colonial Capitals of the Dominion of Virginia*, she watched from her doorway as British Colonel Tarleton and his dragoons rode through the town during the summer of 1781 and "cursed them until they were out of sight."

Another story from Foster concerns Lucy Paradise, the daughter of Philip Ludwell and one of the wealthiest heiresses in the colony. She and her husband traveled much between Virginia and England, entertaining people such as Samuel Johnson, Oliver Goldsmith, and Sir Joshua Reynolds while in London. The story tells that the day she met George Washington in person for the first time, his height and looks impressed her so mightily, she went home and beat her husband "because he was so small and ugly."

The city continued to grow and develop during the next several decades as the colony's capital. In 1746, however, the capitol burned, leaving little more than a charred shell. A debate began in the colony, urged especially by representatives from more westerly counties, about moving the capital to a more central location. After considerable debate and a series of proposals from different locations asking the capital to be located in their region, the Assembly voted to reconstruct the capitol building, keeping Williamsburg as Virginia's capital for the time being. However, periodic proposals for removal of the capital to a location more central to the rapidly-expanding colony appeared in subsequent meetings of the Assembly, leading Williamsburg area representatives to be on guard against such proposals.

During the first half of the eighteenth century, Williamsburg's population, about 1,500 people of a roughly equal racial and sexual balance, developed a capital town of which several observers noted its harmony and unity according to the rationalist principles of town planning and development then prevalent in the Atlantic world. The people who inhabited the town contributed to its success and effectiveness. Its participation in the British Empire, however, even if unrecognized by 1750, lay the foundation for dramatic changes that altered drastically Williamsburg's future for the worse after 1780.

Chapter Four

WILLIAMSBURG DURING THE REVOLUTIONARY ERA

Between 1754 and 1781 Williamsburg was a center of confrontations and war between the British and French colonies, and then between the British colonies and Great Britain respectively. The city achieved maturity by 1750 as a political capital. Numerous Virginians looked to the British government, in the person of the lieutenant governor or royal governor, to advance their interests. Virginia, based on her 1609 colonial charter revision, claimed a vast expanse of territory bordered in 1750 on the west by the Mississippi River, the north by the Great Lakes, the south by the Virginia–North Carolina border extended to the Mississippi, and a line from the mouth of the Potomac River northwest to the Great Lakes. The territory came to be known as the Old Northwest Territory.

During the 1740s a number of Virginians, aided by political allies in England's colonial and royal bureaucracies, formed land companies and sought major acreages, numbering in the hundreds of thousands, in the valleys of or west of the Appalachian Mountains, especially in the Ohio River valley.

Among those Virginians staking such claims was George Washington. Washington, ambitious to enter into Virginia's top social rank, used his friendship with Lord Fairfax's family and his connections through his older half-brother Lawrence to advance his interests. Washington was a land speculator even during his youth. The Ohio Company, which he joined as a young man, and other land companies in Virginia and other colonies, sought and obtained sizeable land grants in the upper Ohio River valley. Formed in 1748, the Ohio Company conducted its official business from Williamsburg, although its actual interests were in acquiring lands across the Appalachians.

French fur-trading interests and Ohio Indian resistance confronted ambitious Virginians. The French, from their St. Lawrence River and lower Mississippi (New Orleans and other towns in or near the Mississippi delta) colonies, tried to block English westward expansion. From Quebec City they sent parties to strengthen their claims to the upper Ohio River, build forts in that region, and create alliances with Ohio native populations. French expeditions led by such figures as Céloron de Blainville traversed the Ohio area between 1751 and 1753, securing France's hold on the region.

Iroquois Confederation leaders also tested their claims to the Ohio country, having long been overlords for various Ohio native groups. Competition between English and French interests for the allegiance of the Iroquois allowed them to be neutral and diplomatic go-betweens in negotiations concerning the future of the Ohio country.

George Washington and a newly-arrived lieutenant-governor, Robert Dinwiddie, met in Williamsburg in the early 1750s to discuss how best to confront the French threat. Unlike many of his predecessors, Dinwiddie was not a career army officer. Arriving in Williamsburg on November 20, 1751, he had instructions to protect Virginia's claim to lands west of the mountains. Washington, just entering his twenties, wanted an aggressive English policy to expel the French from the Ohio. Dinwiddie, agreeing with the young officer, sent him in 1753 with instructions to confront French officials at the Forks of the Ohio (modern-day Pittsburgh) and order them to return to Canada. Washington journeyed overland in the winter of 1753–1754, killed a French diplomat, received the French refusal to retreat, and signed a French document admitting that he had deliberately murdered the diplomat (Washington had no knowledge of French and neither did those who accompanied him—he always claimed he had been duped into signing the document).

The following summer Washington, leading a small contingent of troops, returned to the region only to be defeated near the Forks and forced to return to Williamsburg where he informed Dinwiddie of his failure. The English then began war against the French in the Ohio, a war that grew into a world war for empire. Called the French and Indian War in North America, it was also known as the Seven Years' War in Europe. Since it was fought all over the world (African coastlines, India, the West Indies, North America, the high seas, and Europe), it also has the title of the Great War for Empire. Lasting from 1754 (in North America) until 1763, the war cost England approximately £137 million sterling.

Williamsburg remained a center of military activity during the war. As colonial Virginia's capital, the city had many British officers and civilian officials pass through or remain in it temporarily as they carried out their assignments respecting England's western frontiers. The English and colonials received a severe drubbing in the Ohio valley until English Indian agents negotiated switches from French to English allegiance of Ohio and Iroquois Indians. By 1758 and 1759, however, the military focus in North America shifted from the Ohio valley to the St. Lawrence as British and colonial armies attacked French forces in Canada's two major cities, Quebec and Montreal. When the war ended in 1763, Britain and her colonies forced France to cede all her North American territories. The English took most of modern-day

Williamsburg

Canada and all lands east of the Mississippi, including Florida (a Spanish possession until the peace).

Although a major success for England and Virginia, the war left many sources of friction between them. England's officials desperately needed ways to reduce the enormous national debt from the war and to administer the vast new empire conquered from France and Spain. During the war Virginians issued paper currency to pay ongoing military expenses and English merchants did not want to accept inflated paper money for debts Virginia planters owed them. Friction between English military and civilian officers and bureaucrats and their Virginia counterparts added to growing suspicion and distrust between the two.

Yet in 1760, when George III (1760–1820) ascended the English throne and again in 1763 when news of the end of the war (Treaty of Paris in 1763) reached Williamsburg, the city put on elaborate celebrations including balls, grand illuminations of the public buildings and many private houses, parades, and fireworks. Williamsburg residents, like their counterparts in other cities and in the countryside of all the colonies, gloried in the greatness of the British Empire. Few thought that twelve years later they would be engaged in a struggle leading to a declaration of independence from that empire. Yet even before the outbreak of the Great War for Empire there were more thoughtful observers like Pehr Kalm, touring North America on behalf of the Swedish government in 1749, who remarked on the likelihood that colonials would become independent within twenty-five to thirty years. Other travelers indicated similar thoughts in the early 1750s.

Williamsburg residents, however, generally liked being members of the British Empire. The city's inhabitants engaged in government, artisanship, or merchandizing, generally. With a concentration of educated leaders living in or near Williamsburg and House of Burgesses' members augmenting that number during regular meetings of the Assembly, the city had a cosmopolitan feel to it. Generally residents got on well with the lieutenant governor or governor (after royal governors had to live in Virginia), even during political crises preceding independence. Assembly journals and the city's *Virginia Gazette* provide extant documentary testimonies to the regard with which Virginians held their governors after 1763.

Before 1750 British colonial officials debated changes in colonial policy, changes delayed until the end of the Great War for Empire. These might have provoked resistance in and of themselves, but the need to pay war expenses and new administrative costs brought stiff resistance from Virginians, voiced through assembly meetings at Williamsburg. The House of Burgesses wrote and dispatched to England remonstrances, memorials, petitions, and official letters protesting significant Parliamentary changes in policy or laying of taxes on colonial Virginians. Royal governors in Williamsburg on occasion connived with colonials to evade royal instructions or policy changes.

For instance, several governors aided colonial Virginians in evading the Proclamation of 1763 by which George III forbade temporarily the settlement of colonists west of the Appalachian Mountains. English officials needed time to negotiate with Indians to surrender their lands. To many Virginians, the whole purpose of the French and Indian War was to take control of the west to settle it.

Governor Francis Fauquier arrived in Williamsburg in 1758 to replace Dinwiddie, and spent time dealing with Virginians' concerns about the west. During the latter phases of the French and Indian War, Fauquier participated in treaty negotiations with western natives to obtain English claims to lands. He led Virginians in war that broke out between English and Indians (called Pontiac's War) in 1763–1764. He advised Virginians on how to defy the Proclamation Line of 1763. He and later governors participated in treaty-making sessions during the later 1760s. All this Fauquier did from Williamsburg, now the provincial capital of a vast western empire.

Williamsburg's regard for her governors notwithstanding, the House of Burgesses formally protested a 1765 extension of the English stamp tax to the colonies, argued against the Townshend Duties of 1767, and made plans for and carried out an association to prevent the sale and use of imported English goods among Virginians. When Parliament repealed a new tax law in response to colonial protests, city leaders staged a major celebration thanking the English government for the repeal and rehearsing their love for and affinity to England. Other English policy changes such as attempts to transport accused smugglers to England or some other colony for trial brought protests from Virginians, usually through the city as the seat of the Assembly. Efforts at quartering British soldiers among the colonists also brought protests from the Assembly, meeting in the city. Those resisting English policy between 1763 and 1776 launched official protests through the Assembly as it sat in the capitol during regular sessions.

At the same time, many in the city remained loyal to England and expressed their loyalty as openly as they could. Whigs (as those resistant to English policy were called) suppressed Tory (loyalists before the War for Independence) sentiment, using techniques ranging from public shaming in the *Virginia Gazette* to threats of or actual carrying out of tarring and feathering. City Tories questioned the level of rhetoric and the passionate displays of resistance that Whig orators and writers demonstrated in the 1760s and early 1770s. For example, the October 1764 session of the House of Burgesses dispatched an address to George III, a memorial to the House of Lords, and a remonstrance to the House of Commons protesting the Stamp Act bill before Parliament at the time, claiming that colonials were being taxed without their consent. The statements claimed that only the Virginia Assembly could legitimately tax Virginia colonials. These were the sentiments of the more famous resolves Patrick Henry introduced at the end of the May 1765 session of the House of Burgesses, examples that differed from the earlier statements only in their intemperance of language.

Royal governors Fauquier, Botetourt (1770–1772), and Dunmore (1773–1776) did much to placate Virginians, especially those powerful figures living in or around Williamsburg. Yet when Assembly sessions became too threatening or the language too intemperate, they had only one choice—to prorogue or dissolve the Assembly (the latter requiring new elections for the House of Burgesses).

When dissolutions occurred, Whig leaders assembled in the Apollo Room of the Raleigh Tavern on Duke of Gloucester Street to continue planning resistance and finding ways to carry it out against British policy. It was in the Apollo Room that plans for the Continental Association (a response to the Townshend Act of 1767) were made. Ironically, however, as colonial leaders spoke of freedom and attacked what they called tyranny, sales of slaves continued to take place in front of the Raleigh.

As political resistance developed during the 1760s and 1770s, the city itself continued to grow and develop. Marked as an attractive and pleasing town to visit, the City of Williamsburg displayed a thoughtful plan, even if modified during the decades after its foundation. New shops appeared, new houses were constructed, and new public buildings arose in the third quarter of the eighteenth century. In order to aid the construction programs, the Assembly in 1769 firmly defined York–James City Counties' boundary within the city to make clear where York and where James City County existed. Duke of Gloucester Street still remained generally the boundary between the two counties, but the Assembly had to pass a special act in order for James City County to construct a new courthouse (part of the restoration called today the Courthouse of 1770). The act traded a York County parcel of land on which the courthouse stands for a similar-sized piece in James City County. That courthouse remained the governmental center for Williamsburg and James City County until 1930, when the restoration bought it.

The colonial government also erected another building, called the Public Hospital (known now as Eastern State Hospital), in this period. Constructed to house the mentally disordered, the hospital opened just two years before Lexington and Concord and the outbreak of the War for Independence. In 1766, Governor Francis Fauquier asked the House of Burgesses to provide money and guidance for the construction of a public hospital. The burgesses endorsed the idea in the form of a resolution, but took no further action at that session, although Fauquier reminded them of their commitment when the session ended in April 1767. Not until 1769, after Fauquier's death, did the burgesses finally approve a design and the money to construct the hospital.

Completed and opened in October 1773, the hospital held thirty patients. Run by a board appointed originally by the burgesses, the hospital served the colony and newly-independent state during the war, although lack of income and inflation forced the staff to close it for four years. The board of fifteen men (all laymen) appointed all the staff, including the keeper and matron, and guards and nurses. Located on the north side of France Street on about four acres of land, the hospital provided food, shelter, treatment, and clothing for its patients. Before a patient could be admitted, an analysis of his assets and income was done to ascertain if the state needed to support him while incarcerated. The hospital's original purpose was to cure patients and rehabilitate them into society, but that aim proved difficult to attain. Hospital staff returned about 20 percent of the inmates to society during the first three decades of operation.

The Burgesses named James Galt first keeper of the hospital; his responsibilities included oversight of patients, the physical plant, and staff members. His wife became matron at the same time. The Galt family remained actively involved with the hospital for the next several decades. They not only provided hospital management, but doctors and surgeons as well. During the War for Independence the hospital remained open, but with few patients due to the danger of British invasion and seizure of Williamsburg. Severe, runaway inflation remained another problem for the hospital. The Assembly never supplied enough money for salaries, food, medicines, or medical staff due to inflation. This situation continued after the war.

The Galts remained fixtures in Williamsburg until the Civil War. Dr. Alexander Galt, son of James Galt, bought the Thomas Nelson house in 1823 and directed the hospital through much of the antebellum era. His son, Dr. John Minson Galt, became the hospital's supervisor on the death of his father. Their home, built sometime before 1718, became Thomas Nelson's Williamsburg house and is located a few doors west of the Benjamin Waller house (see below). Nelson, a part of the Yorktown Nelson family founded by Thomas "Scotch Tom" Nelson, who arrived in Virginia around 1720, was grandson to "Scotch Tom" and son of William. Thomas Nelson signed the Declaration of Independence on behalf of Virginia, was governor of the state during the War for Independence, and commanded Virginia's state forces at the Battle of Yorktown from September to October 1781.

At the time the hospital rose from the ground, the city had about 200 homes, many built near or shortly after mid-century. Along Francis Street, for instance, Benjamin

Williamsburg

Waller's house was completed about 1745. Waller, long-time clerk of the city and James City County, tutored George Wythe and his house remained in Waller hands for three generations. Waller's grandson William married Elizabeth Tyler and granddaughter Eliza married George Blow in 1807.

Custis Square lay next to the public hospital mentioned above. The property of Colonel John Custis passed to his son John Parke Custis, Martha Washington's first husband. George Washington managed the property after he married her, before the war broke out. Martha's ex-father-in-law Colonel Custis corresponded with Peter Collinson, maintaining a lifelong interest in natural history, especially botany.

Another house on Francis Street, at its intersection with England Street, is the Lightfoot house, named for Philip Lightfoot I who built the house sometime around 1730 as his townhouse. It remained in the Lightfoot family until 1786 when Reverend J. Brackenridge bought it. The house became a guest house in 1962 for visiting foreign dignitaries coming to see the restored city. These houses and others like them form the residential cadre that has become the core of the restoration of Williamsburg since the 1920s. Many have been intensively studied as historical and archaeological artifacts of the eighteenth-century city.

One such house is James Geddy's home located on two lots at the northeast intersection of Palace Green and Duke of Gloucester Street. James Geddy I was a gunsmith and brass founder who settled in the city during the 1730s. He built it as his domicile and workshop, a common practice in traditional societies. Active as a smith by the late 1730s, Geddy did not specialize; like so many other colonial artisans, he followed broadly the smithing trade. Although most skilled in gunsmithing and brass founding, he also did silver, gold, and many other forms of smithing during his career. His sons William and David began advertising their own services as smiths in the early 1750s, just a few years after their father's death in 1749. They, like their father, carried on general smith's trade: gunsmithing, brass founding, swordsmithing, bucklemaking, cutlery making, and many other arts of smithing trades.

The house, smithy, and shop complex had to be rebuilt on one lot when Geddy's widow sold the easterly lot in 1750 the year after her husband's death. She conveyed the other lot to her second son, James II. What happened to her other three sons, David, William, and John, is not clear, although William remained in the city until the 1760s. James Geddy II was a silversmith by specialty, but his shop also produced most other goods that a smith might make. He also sold through the shop many smithy products imported from England. Although James Geddy II was evidently making arms for the Patriots during the opening years of the War for Independence, he had left Williamsburg by the end of November 1777, reason or reasons unknown.

Williamsburg During the Revolutionary Era

City residents and visitors alike in the eighteenth century drank substantial amounts of alcohol. Taverns and inns abounded in the city and in the surrounding areas of James City and York Counties. The most popular alcoholic drinks were Madeira wine and a variety of rum punches. Served in places like Wetherburn's Tavern, located on the south side of Duke of Gloucester Street, alcohol gave opportunity for socializing and exchanging news about England and her policies in the inns, ordinaries, and taverns of the late colonial period.

Wetherburn's Tavern was quite popular during the third quarter of the eighteenth century, retaining its popularity during the early years of the War for Independence. At its largest size, the tavern consisted of three portions, totaling almost eighty-five feet in length and about thirty feet in width. Located in the business section of the city, the tavern remained in Wetherburn's hands until 1760 when he died, although when he acquired the establishment is not clear.

Perhaps the most famous story about the tavern concerns what archaeologists found when they dug its foundations in the 1960s, thirty-nine wine bottles filled with cherries (the English black Morello variety) and carefully stoppered. Chemists who analyzed the cherries and liquid contents of the bottles found no sugar, brandy, or any other liquor in them. Why they were buried around the foundation of the tavern's kitchen remains a mystery, but colonials did enjoy the eighteenth-century version of canned cherries and the stems had all been trimmed to the one-quarter-inch length that seemed to colonials to be the most appropriate length for preserving the cherries.

Customers patronizing the city's businesses during pre-Revolutionary days fluctuated according to the city's political and judicial rhythms. When the General Court met in spring and fall and when the Assembly met in late spring and early winter, the town's population swelled. During "Publick Times" the population might grow to 8,000 or even 10,000 from its usual 1,500 to 2,000.

As Williamsburg matured during the third quarter of the eighteenth century, city and colonial leaders made plans for significant changes in the economic system, even as resistance to English policy mounted. Increasing population in and around the city necessitated changes in the transportation structure. Leaders planned new roads to link the city with settlements and communities on the peninsula. Talk of constructing a canal from Jamestown around the western outskirts of the city to Yorktown began. More new ferries crossed creeks and rivers linking the peninsula together and the city more fully into the peninsula. It is true that the city served political and cultural purposes far more than economic, but by the time of independence, the city was also an economic center, the outdoor area called the Exchange being an important example.

Williamsburg

Ship captains, tobacco factors, and planters walked and talked about tobacco prices and issues affecting those prices on the Exchange, an open region just east of the capitol. Ship captains especially had a good idea of what did control tobacco prices, having usually just arrived from England. Tobacco factors, agents for tobacco merchants—usually Scottish—in the British Isles, had less direct knowledge of tobacco prices than did the captains, but they often knew a good deal about influences driving tobacco prices.

Many peninsula planters, however, had already begun turning away from tobacco to general grain. Planting wheat or maize, they looked to the ever-growing number of water mills around Williamsburg to grind their grain. Most peninsula mills were water-powered, but one wind mill existed in the northern part of the city. It ground grain only when the wind blew; thus the miller flew a flag on days the mill opened for grinding. Although the windmill worked only on sufficiently windy days, it did have the advantage of year-round usefulness. During especially cold winters, watermill races froze and the mills had to await the thaw before their usefulness revived.

At the end of the Great War for Empire in 1763, the city and its hinterland enjoyed a maturity and sophistication that many visitors of the time noted. The city had a pleasing vista, was small and open enough to be attractive to all but the most curmudgeonly, and possessed a number of cultural traits that provided concerts, dancing, and plays enough to satisfy most appetites. A theater opened in the city early in the eighteenth century, but quickly closed due to continued Puritanic frowning upon such gaiety and frivolity. By mid-century, however, there was sufficient support for a theater in the city and it remained an important cultural component of Williamsburg life until the Revolution.

When resistance to British policy began in earnest in the 1760s, Williamsburg had reached a level of maturity and sophistication that accorded her residents and those who visited as members of the government the confidence to confront British officials. In May 1763, Fauquier asked the Assembly to place the colony's economy on a more secure footing. No longer could the Assembly vote new issues of paper money to finance the colony's war support. The House responded that it had always been and would always continue to be loyal to His Majesty's government, but claimed that Virginians' rights as British citizens permitted the Assembly to act on such matters in its own right. The result was a Parliamentary act that forbade the colony from issuing paper currency as legal tender. In the meantime British ministers sought new revenues; to do that, they decided to extend to the colonies the English stamp law passed centuries before.

Williamsburg During the Revolutionary Era

Virginians remained steadfastly loyal to England during the 1760s, always insisting however through House of Burgesses meetings in Williamsburg on their own rights and privileges. The House of Burgesses thought of itself as Virginia's House of Commons. Parliament intended the Stamp Act (1765), Townshend Act (1767), and Tea Act (1772) to raise revenues from the colonies to help defray colonial administrative and military costs, and to regulate better the trade between colonies and England. But as Parliament passed each revenue act colonials resisted in various ways. The Stamp Act brought constitutional protests and violent demonstrations. The Townshend Act produced constitutional protests and an economic program of non-importation of all manufactured English goods. The Tea Act brought renewed violence and peaceful protests in the form of days of fasting, humiliation, and prayer.

Virginians participated in all these actions through their legislature, meeting in Williamsburg. But they steadfastly maintained their loyalty to England, beginning expressions of discontent with strong protestations of affection and love for the mother country. But thoughts of differences between colonials and English were never too far below the surface during the 1760s and early 1770s. The city remained a center of political discussion, debate, gossip, and innuendo in those years.

Virginia's leaders, meeting in the city at the capitol building every few months, were politically savvy and understood as well as English administrators how to manipulate the system. Although many issues and confrontations developed between the House of Burgesses and the governor during the 1760s and 1770s, there was still harmony between the two symbols of government and authority.

Between 1763 and 1776, however, tension and friction slowly eroded that harmony between representatives of the people's will and royal authority. Each successive dispute between the colonies and royal or Parliamentary authority heightened levels of suspicion on each side's part. The Stamp Act crisis of 1764–1766, the Townshend Act crisis of 1766–1768, the Boston Massacre of 1770, the burning of the Gaspé in 1772, the Tea Act and reaction to it in 1772–1774, and creation of two Continental Congresses lead eventually to the Declaration of Independence; they combined to define and refine political, constitutional, and cultural differences separating colonists and English.

As tensions mounted, however, relations between city leaders and royal officials remained cordial, sometimes quite friendly. Royal governors aided Williamsburgers as they sought to acquire lands in or west of the Appalachian Mountains. Personal relationships developed between colonial Virginians and English officials, relations that often lay the foundation for the future greatness of the individual Virginian.

Williamsburg

Thomas Jefferson came to The College of William and Mary in the early 1760s as a student. Born in 1743, Jefferson's father was Peter Jefferson, one of the surveyors who, with Joshua Frye, created the map of the Chesapeake colonies known as the Frye-Jefferson map, first published in 1755. Peter Jefferson, like Washington's father, was not of the highest levels of Virginia planters. Jefferson's mother, however, was a Randolph, one of the first-level families (formerly known as the First Families of Virginia or FFVs) of the colony. Thomas Jefferson demonstrated early that he had a strong intellect. Admitted to William and Mary and quickly showing his intellectual brilliance, Jefferson found himself admitted as an undergraduate student to the company of William Small, professor of mathematics, George Wythe, professor of law and one of Jefferson's tutors, and Governor Francis Fauquier. Small, Wythe, and Fauquier dined together frequently and discussed a variety of Enlightenment topics as well as the latest news and gossip. Long before he left William and Mary, Jefferson became a fourth in that company. Even so, despite his affection for Small and Fauquier, Jefferson soon entered the Whig cause and, because he had felicity with written English, became one of the principal pens of the Whig, then revolutionary, movements.

George Washington had a friendship with Lord Dunmore, the last royal governor of Virginia and a man whom Virginians came to hate because he offered freedom to Virginia slaves who fled their masters to join British forces during the violence and turmoil immediately preceding the War for Independence. Washington and Dunmore often met for breakfast at Dunmore's farm just outside Williamsburg when Washington was in town for Assembly or other meetings.

The complex human relations in the city preceding the war are reflected in continuing friendships and cordial associations among leading figures often publicly at odds with each other. City residents, as in Virginia and the rest of the colonies generally, made decisions for or against independence in the years between 1773 or 1774, and 1776. Many sought to remain neutral, hoping to escape the turmoil and violence, perhaps, or not wanting to make a decision one way or the other until they knew which way the wind blew.

But in the early 1770s, however, tensions relaxed. Then Parliament decided that to save the British East India Company from bankruptcy it would pass a Tea Act. The East India Company was unable to sell the enormous supply of tea it had in its London warehouses and was threatened with bankruptcy. The tea tax from the Townshend Acts was retained after repeal of the rest of the duties, but had done little good in replenishing English finances. When Parliament repealed the Townshend duties except the tax on tea, Norfolk, Virginia merchants led by Andrew Sproule gathered in Williamsburg in June 1770 to form a group called the Association to boycott the import of tea and other British goods. The House of Burgesses joined the protest, asking each Virginia county to create a five-man committee to enforce the association Sproule and his associates created.

In the meantime, colonial smugglers illegally imported Dutch tea. The 1772 Tea Act lowered the duty on East India Company tea to undercut such smugglers. Parliament also hoped to reduce the enormous tea surpluses in the Company's warehouses. Finally, the act gave the company a monopoly of colonial sales to further reduce the surplus.

Colonials, prodded by smugglers, decried the monopoly and made plans to refuse the tea. Parliament, however, made it impossible to send back the tea without first unloading it and forcing colonial merchants to pay import duties on it. Protests mounted and, in 1773 when the first tea ships began arriving in colonial harbors, violence ensued against property, not persons. This time Parliament's reaction to colonial violence, including the Boston Tea Party and similar incidents in other colonies—Virginia included—brought matters to a head between 1774 and 1776.

As Anglo-Virginia relations once again deteriorated by the summer of 1772, a few Virginia Whigs, led by Thomas Jefferson, Patrick Henry, Richard Henry Lee, and Francis Lightfoot Lee, established a Committee of Correspondence to maintain close contact with other colonies. This committee between that summer and 1776 evolved into a shadow government. The committee collected, analyzed, and disseminated information and calls for action, especially resistance to the new Tea Act. Once the Boston and other tea parties occurred and Parliament reacted with the legislation called collectively by colonials the Intolerable Acts, these committees of correspondence, often meeting secretly in colonial capitals like Williamsburg, directed Whig resistance.

In Williamsburg Lord Dunmore, the last royal governor of Virginia (who had arrived in 1770), remained a popular figure until the crisis that began in 1773 produced the independence movement. His wife and children came to Virginia in spring 1774 and the governor promptly entered his three eldest sons in the College of William and Mary. The city welcomed the governor's family with its usual celebrations of balls and dinners. In the spring of 1775, however, Dunmore and Whig leaders fell out over his orders to seize the powder, arms, and munitions stored in the magazine in Williamsburg.

Early on the morning of April 20, 1775, just one day after Lexington and Concord in Massachusetts, Captain Henry Collins with a squad of British sailors (there were no British soldiers in Virginia at the time) took all the stores from the magazine they could crowd into one of the governor's wagons. The sailors escorted the wagon to a dock where the munitions were moved to a British warship. The city erupted with threats of violence and armed resistance to British policy. Only when Richard Corbin, the king's deputy receiver general, paid Carter Braxton, representing the Whigs, a bill of exchange for the powder did things begin to quiet in the city. Patrick Henry, who raised a sizeable militia force to take back forcibly the powder, kept the force in being after the payment and Dunmore then declared him an outlaw. Dunmore then wrote the mayor of Williamsburg, Dr. William Pasteur, that if any harm came to him or his family, he would burn the city and issue a proclamation freeing all slaves in Virginia.

From that moment on, relations between British and Virginia Whigs deteriorated until full-scale fighting broke out and Virginia declared her independence. Although English ships and troops menaced Williamsburg during 1775 and 1776, city leaders and Virginia Whigs generally used Williamsburg as their center of resistance. Those loyal to England, like John Randolph, the colony's last royal attorney general, usually passed through the city on their way to British warships as they made their way to England, the British West Indies, or Canada. Many Loyalists, however, chose to remain in the colony, taking oaths not to confront the Patriots as violence escalated into war. They remained on their farms or estates to try to protect them from Patriot confiscation, although that strategy did not always succeed.

How complex personal relations had become is demonstrated by the fact that the evening before the magazine incident Washington had dinner with the governor. The next morning the two rode out to Dunmore's farm, breakfasted, and discussed events. Washington must have known of the seizure and there must have been some mention of the powder incident, but relations between the two remained cordial for several months thereafter.

By mid-May 1775, Dunmore's family had taken up residence aboard HMS *Fowey* and British sailors were stationed in the Governor's Palace to protect the governor. By summer 1775, British and colonials were engaged in war as the siege of Boston began. As the Second Continental Congress got under way in Philadelphia, Dunmore still called the Assembly into session and it began meeting on June 1. When the members heard that Dunmore himself had gone aboard the *Fowey*, they continued to meet, not adjourning until June 20, by which time they had rejected King George III's Olive Branch petition. At the same time, Virginia's Third Convention began meeting and functioned as an open government.

The Assembly reconvened in May 1776, but the House of Burgesses had so few members attending that the clerk simply wrote FINIS across the last page and an institution begun in 1619 ended, replaced shortly thereafter by the House of Delegates.

Dunmore and his ships moved to Norfolk, where he took up command of forces opposed to the rebels, as they were then called. On December 9, 1775, he and his men fought the engagement known as the Battle of Great Bridge. Williamsburg was the staging point for Virginia's troops under the command of Major-General Charles Lee, who spent about two months in and around Williamsburg training and equipping the troops for the fight.

As the war began, Williamsburg remained Virginia's capital; the possibility of British attack remained, however, a constant threat. Virginia Patriots held several conventions to debate and plan their political, military, diplomatic, and constitutional strategies. The early conventions, beginning in summer 1774, met in Williamsburg and drew representatives from all over the colony, just as colonial Assembly meetings had. The conventions, however, had no legal or constitutional authority until Patriots had written and approved a state constitution for the newly-independent state.

The capital remained in Williamsburg until 1780 when the state's assembly moved it to Richmond. Planning and transition of Virginia from colony to state occurred in Williamsburg during those five years. English prisoners taken in battles in the Old Northwest were sent to Williamsburg, including the English commander Colonel Henry Hamilton, called "Hairbuyer" because he offered bounties to Native-Americans for Patriot scalps, a practice colonials had long condoned and practiced themselves. In 1779, the Virginia state assembly created the counties of Kentucky and Illinois respectively. But the Assembly that year, responding to fears the British might just do what they were to do in 1781 and to repeated calls for a more centrally-located capital from western representatives, voted to remove the capital to Richmond. By spring 1780, all executive offices had moved to Richmond and on May 1, 1780, the Assembly held its first formal legislative session in the new capital. Williamsburg entered into a long period of decline and stagnation. The city continued as county seat for James City County, but within a surprisingly short period of time, most artisans and craftsmen had left the city.

Militarily, however, between 1776 and 1780, British forces occasionally raided Virginia; not until spring 1781 did they mount the long-anticipated invasion. Lord Charles Cornwallis, British commander in the southern region, sent advance forces led by Banastre Tarleton and Benedict Arnold into Virginia in spring 1781.

In April 1781, Tarleton's and Arnold's forces attacked and destroyed a shipyard on the Chickahominy River, appropriated by Patriots at the beginning of the war to build naval vessels to protect Virginia waters. By the end of April, British forces secured control of Williamsburg and its surrounding territory. Patriot forces retreated toward Richmond to protect the new capital as best they could.

Williamsburg

Cornwallis followed later with his main army. He wanted to use the excellent harbor at Yorktown as a maritime center from which to conduct raids on Virginia tobacco farms and plantations in the Tidewater region. Using Yorktown, which could be easily re-supplied from British-held New York City, Cornwallis believed he would be able to reduce Virginia resistance and strike at the heart of Patriot support. But before he moved to Yorktown, he conducted several movements in the peninsula and Southside during late spring and early summer with Williamsburg as one of his focal points.

He chose Williamsburg as camp in late June and July before setting out for Portsmouth across the James River near the end of July. During late June, his forces skirmished and fought a small contingent led by the Marquis de Lafayette at the battle of Green Spring, just outside the city. The opposing forces first fought at Spencer's Ordinary near Centerville, but on June 26 an intense engagement resulted in over 150 casualties. Between then and July 6, the forces continued maneuvering around Williamsburg until Cornwallis decided to move his forces to Portsmouth preliminary to the move to Yorktown. Cornwallis conducted a feint in which he made it appear to Lafayette that his main force had already crossed the James River. Then he drew Lafayette's force into the trap on July 6. Only when Lafayette got to some high ground overlooking Jamestown and the whole Green Spring battlefield did he realize the trap Cornwallis had set for him. He immediately ordered his forces to retreat; Cornwallis continued his movement across the James.

Cornwallis thought about returning to New York City, but decided in July 1781 to establish his permanent camp at Yorktown. Moving there in mid-summer, he set the stage for the Battle of Yorktown. Cornwallis believed the British Navy would keep open sea lanes between the Chesapeake and New York City, but on September 5, 1781, his assumption fell apart. A French fleet successfully attacked and drove off a British fleet coming to the bay to re-supply him. The French navy thus controlled the bay and allowed Washington's forced march and a slower move of the French army to surround Cornwallis at Yorktown. Instead of the town being his point of attack, it became a town besieged between mid-September and the surrender date in October. Cornwallis's surrender brought an end to the last major campaign of the war. Over the winter of 1781–1782, Williamsburg remained a hospital and convalescent center for the allied armies. But the town's decline had already set in. During the next several decades, the town became a stagnant, sleepy community.

War-time and post-war descriptions of Williamsburg and its surrounding area indicate much destruction. The war left much property ruined. Plantations and farms around the city were damaged extensively or destroyed, especially during the summer

1781 campaign. Williamsburg itself suffered extensive damage, with some buildings burned either partially or completely. The town rebuilt only slowly, in fact some buildings like the Governor's Palace and the capitol slowly deteriorated until they became unrecognizable wrecks by the mid-nineteenth century. Williamsburg entered into a long era of inactivity, sleepiness, stagnation, and decline. Not until the twentieth century did the city rebound from the devastating loss of her status as capital.

Chapter Five

AFTER 1783: BETWEEN THE REVOLUTION AND CIVIL WAR

At the end of the Revolutionary War, Williamsburg underwent a prolonged decline due mostly to the transfer of Virginia's capital from the city to Richmond. Substantial war damage, post-war nationwide depression, and fire contributed to Williamsburg's decline, also. The city was James City County's seat, but the loss of governmental offices to Richmond encouraged many craftsmen, professionals, and businesses, especially taverns and inns, to move to the new capital.

Williamsburg had to find alternative economic sources if it was to survive, but it generally failed to do so, remaining a town on the brink of economic collapse during the nineteenth century, except for the Civil War era. Between the Revolutionary and Civil Wars, the city sought to capitalize on tourism (1807 and 1857) and the beginnings of the great transportation changes that came over the United States. With the exception of a brief flurry of interest attendant on the two commemorations of the founding of Virginia at Jamestown (just a few miles from Williamsburg), little came of the efforts at economic revival. The town became somnolent, according to some observers and local historians. The city had passed almost into a coma in the eyes of others.

The college, mental hospital, market town, and county seat remained the city's principal sources of income during the antebellum years. With the exception of the two institutions, the city, a small, sleepy town, became the seat of a rural, southern county in the midst of a rural region that had few prospects. Population remained steady during the antebellum period, but wealthy families who had either called the city home or had city houses for purposes of entertaining during the colonial era drifted away. Lands that produced substantial quantities of tobacco in the late colonial era lost their fertility and only with significant agricultural change did fertility return.

As with the rest of the east coast, Williamsburg had to adjust to peace in 1783. Once the announcement of peace had been formally made, Williamsburg staged a parade through town to celebrate the event. The parade consisted of the mayor and common council, a sergeant carrying the city's mace, a herald to read the proclamation of peace as the procession wound through the town, and many townspeople. According to one source, when the parade ended, the participants made their way to the Raleigh Tavern to slake their thirst after the long, dusty walk.

After 1783: Between the Revolution and Civil War

On a more somber note, several townsmen who died in battle or military camps during the war had widows and children needing support. Also, some of the city and surrounding countryside had to be rebuilt due to destruction during Cornwallis's campaign in the summer of 1781. But partially-destroyed public buildings no longer needed (such as the Governor's Palace and capitol) remained untouched after the war's end, lending a romantic air of decay to the city, an air that travelers of a poetic bent often caught in the next twenty-five or thirty years.

Similar problems affected the residents of James City County, suggesting that the city's difficulties, while common in eastern Virginia, would plague the town for years after the war. In addition to the destruction wrought by the conflicting armies, disease and insect invasions also occurred. For the first several years after peace came, Williamsburg and its environs faced hardship. The city lost its glitter, the county its wealth. Roughly half the colonial population disappeared after 1783.

Governmentally, few changes occurred at the local level, but at the newly-created state level a system of state-wide taxation, instituted in 1782, brought lists of property-owners that can now be used to acquire a better understanding of the distribution and evaluation of wealth in the city. The assessors listed personal and real property, evaluating items state law required be enumerated. Incomes in 1780s and 1790s Williamsburg were so low, however, that many individuals found it difficult to pay their assessed taxes. Citizens asked that they be allowed to pay them when they could afford to; some local historians think a few citizens may have asked their slaves to steal for them.

In addition to changes in taxation policy, the state also required localities to maintain a militia force composed of all able-bodied free white men sixteen or over. The militia was to be the first line of defense in case of attack (a threat all through the 1780s and 1790s as major European powers watched closely to see if the new United States might be vulnerable or unable to achieve unity). The local militias also performed public services such as tearing down defensive fortifications around Yorktown and cleaning up what the armies left undone after their departure.

Life, however, slowly settled into the rural routine by which Williamsburg became a small town county seat as the new century began. By the turn of the nineteenth century, the city readjusted to its losses and became a town of about 1,200 to 1,500 whites and African Americans, a figure that would remain steady until 1850 when some economic growth began.

Descriptions of the city in those years immediately after the War for Independence differ; some call Williamsburg depressed, while others refer to it as a clean and wholesome community. Jedidiah Morse, father of Samuel F.B. Morse, visited the city

Williamsburg

from his native New England in 1792. In his description of the town, he called it "dull, forsaken, and melancholy," concluding that removal of the capital to Richmond had "contributed much to the decline of this city." St. George Tucker, lately arrived to Williamsburg from his native Bermuda, retorted that there were "many comfortable houses . . . and still some neat gardens and pleasant situations. . . ." He concluded that few towns could "boast a more pleasant situation, more respectable inhabitants, or a more agreeable and friendly society." Regardless of the town's condition in the 1790s, there was considerable deterioration, especially of the public buildings no longer needed since the removal of the capital. The citizenry permitted the deterioration of those buildings to continue, often until they disappeared.

The Governor's Palace burned in December 1781, after having been used as a military hospital during the Yorktown campaign that fall. The building's remains continued to deteriorate, although the two wing buildings in the front survived the fire and were used for a variety of purposes, including dwellings, during the nineteenth century. Whatever was left of the building was later destroyed and its still-useable bricks sold. By the mid-1830s there was hardly a trace of the building left on the site.

The capitol building began to collapse and by the early 1790s significant portions of it were razed. Fire destroyed much of the rest of the building in the 1830s. The Williamsburg Female Academy was established on the site in 1849 and remained in operation until the Civil War. Few if any of the city's public buildings left from the colonial era survived unhurt into the nineteenth century.

The Raleigh Tavern deteriorated over time after the Revolution, but missed being consumed in a large fire in the city near it in 1842. Although still in use by 1850, the building was slowly rotting away, according to people who stayed in it. Fire finally caught up with the old tavern in December 1859 when the building was completely destroyed. Used as a girls' school and pub before then, the Raleigh's destruction completed the decay of most of the buildings that witnessed important events in the colonial and Revolutionary eras. It was especially the decay of the palace, capitol, the Raleigh, and other colonial attractions that gave Williamsburg its romantic aura in the nineteenth century.

In 1807 and 1857 there were commemorations of the 200th and 250th anniversaries of Jamestown's founding. The original colonial capital, the town virtually disappeared by the mid-eighteenth century and, by the early nineteenth century, Jamestown was little more than a few plantations and the ruins of the seventeenth-century town. The nineteenth-century commemorations brought lots of visitors, many of whom stayed in Williamsburg. The city welcomed the visitors, but failed to develop sustained forms of tourism in the years between the two events.

After 1783: Between the Revolution and Civil War

The 1807 commemoration was not well recorded for posterity, but the usual speeches were given, and speakers included some William and Mary students. Not much was left of the old Jamestown; some believed that ruins they saw were those of the original English intruders, but they might just as well have been left from much later times. Fifty years later, the 1857 commemoration was far better recorded, including even some illustrations used on the cover of *Harper's Weekly* showing Jamestown's ruins. Several thousand visitors arrived in May aboard steamers from Washington, Richmond, Baltimore, and other bay and tributary river cities and towns for the festivities. A hot day, according to some who left written records of their attendance, as in 1807 there was not much to see other than ruins, which souvenir hunters quickly took advantage of by breaking off pieces of bricks, mortar, and tombstones before they reembarked for home. Some of those who remained overnight doubtless stayed in Williamsburg. There were dinners and drinks for those who did stay.

The college and hospital, two institutions on which part of the city's economy depended, had their ups and downs during the decades between the Revolution and Civil War. William and Mary suffered a perennial problem, then and now, of a serious shortage of funds. Revenues from the Crown and Church of England, mainstay incomes during the colonial era, were now cut off. To replace some of those lost revenues, the Assembly allowed the college to begin selling off lands it did not need for its planned growth. Salaries for the president and professors doubtless remained quite low; the situation for the college did not alter that much before the Civil War.

Shortly after the Revolution, James Madison (cousin of the fourth U.S. President) became president of the college and rector of Bruton Parish Church. He was also professor of natural philosophy (an eighteenth-century term for natural scientist–biologist). Some townsmen alleged that he had become a freethinker or had even rejected completely the Christian faith by the time he died in 1812. In 1790 Bishop Madison (as he was known to distinguish him from his more famous cousin the President) became Virginia's first Episcopal bishop (the Church of England became the Episcopal Church in the new nation). Popular and inclined to rationalism and Enlightened thought, Bishop Madison made William and Mary a skeptical institution, especially when the Divinity School was disbanded as Virginia and the nation abolished established religions.

A series of presidents, most of whom also held the position of rector of Bruton Parish Church, succeeded Bishop Madison. Many in the town believed that the college would die along with him in 1812, but it managed to survive; however, it had only a few students and a severely constrained budget. Virginia's militia used the Wren building for part of 1813 as a barracks during the War of 1812. Deterioration of the buildings, due in part to student vandalism and in part simply to lack of maintenance monies, necessitated substantial repairs after 1815. Enrollments waxed and waned during the 1820s and 1830s; the law school, founded by George Wythe during the War for Independence and a replacement for the Divinity School, provided legal education as the law began to professionalize in the United States after 1815. Despite gloomy predictions of some after the War of 1812, the college sustained itself and even grew some.

The college held its own during the 1830s and 1840s, especially under President Thomas Roderick Dew who died suddenly in 1846. Dew, made president in 1836, had been professor before assuming the duties of president and was popular in both capacities. However, an unfortunate choice of a successor to Dew brought troubles to William and Mary and, as a result, it actually had to shut down for a year after the board of visitors demanded that the whole faculty resign. Only with the appointment of Benjamin Stoddart Ewell in 1848 did the college once again gain an able hand to direct its affairs. Through the 1850s, the Civil War, and the immediate aftermath of the war, Ewell kept the college open (except for some of the war years themselves) and promoted its interests. William and Mary, throughout this whole period, remained a private college, needing a good deal of extra funding to supplement the tuition and other expenses students paid.

Ewell devoted over thirty-five years of his life to the college, interrupted only by the Civil War. He attended the United States Military Academy at West Point and evidently hoped to serve in the Army as a career, but that was thwarted. He taught mathematics at William and Mary, one of the subjects he excelled in at West Point. He began teaching mathematics at West Point after his graduation, then taught the subject at Hampden-Sydney and Washington (now Washington & Lee) Colleges. He was one of the first college presidents who was not also rector of Bruton Parish Church.

One of the many crises he had to deal with during the antebellum era was the burning of the main building in 1859. Using the $20,000 insurance money, plus over $35,000 raised by him and the board of visitors, Ewell was able to have the building reconstructed by the time the Civil War broke out. Built in an Italianate style, the building looked little like its colonial predecessor. It had barely begun to serve as a college building when it became a military hospital and barracks early in the Civil War, then burned again, partially in 1862 and fully in 1863.

The college employed a number of people over and above the faculty and president. A bursar, cooks, maintenance staff, and other personnel worked for the college, depending on the ups and downs of the institution before the Civil War. With the Wren building burnt in 1859, rebuilt by 1861, and burnt again during the war, the college experienced many vicissitudes.

Connected with the college is the story of Williamsburg's first Christmas tree. Charles Minnegerode, brought to William and Mary as professor of modern languages and literature in the early 1840s, came from German regions of Europe where the Christmas tree tradition dated to the time of Martin Luther. For the first holidays he celebrated in town he erected in one of his host's smaller rooms a Christmas tree, having the children make colored paper decorations and using remains of candles to adorn it. The tree became so popular with neighborhood children that it soon became a tradition in many households.

The other institution that employed several people in the city, the asylum, also experienced ups and downs. Finished just before the Revolutionary War began, it experienced revenue problems similar to the college's during and immediately after the Revolutionary War. Unlike the college, it was a state-supported institution and once the state government recovered from the effects of the war, it could better support the asylum. The Galt family continued to supervise and control the asylum until the Civil War. They improved treatment, tried to cure patients rather than lock them away, and encouraged them to take an interest and more active role in their own recovery. The Galts encouraged patients to participate in games, both indoor and outdoor. Many gardened, if such activity helped them gain a better sense of their problems and how to deal with them. The last Dr. Galt died in 1862 and the asylum needed a new family dedicated to the care and cure (or attempted cure) of patients. The war interrupted the hospital's development, as it did all development in the town.

Bruton Parish Church lost its position as Virginia's social and religious arbiter after the Revolution, but it remained a central institution of Williamsburg, although its importance and centrality to the city changed dramatically. The church responded more and more to the personality of its rector than it had during the colonial era when it was a central part of the colony's social and cultural system. Disestablishment made Bruton Parish Church religiously and financially equal with all other churches and religions in the new state, and the church building itself experienced the same decline in maintenance and upkeep other public and private buildings did in the city after the War. In consequence, the church's upkeep responded to the vitality and interest of the current rector, to the rhythm of the rectors, and their abilities and interests in maintaining the edifice and its interior. The rectors also usually served as William and Mary's president, thus they divided their time between their church and college duties and responsibilities.

Williamsburg

Three separate legislative acts (1787, 1799, 1802) contributed to the church's troubles in Williamsburg, as those acts provided for the confiscation and sale of the church's glebe lands (lands set aside for rectors to use for income independent of their salaries from the congregation). Confiscation of the glebe lands left Bruton Parish Church without outside sources of income. Most had to come from congregant donations and gifts after 1802. Many of the wealthier members lost much or all of their fortunes and estates in the Revolution, further depleting the church's income. It took until the mid-1830s before the congregation had sufficient monies that it could vote to divide the existing interior into halves in order to create a Sunday school in part of the building. The renovation destroyed the interior symmetry by removing the chancel, the high pulpit, and colonial pews. The chancel, which had graves of people like Orlando Jones and many of the Blair family, was installed on the newly-created wall. All this was once again altered dramatically in a restoration of the church in 1905–1907. If lack of state support, economic stagnation, and population loss meant hard times for Williamsburg, so too did war.

The city and peninsula are areas of the eastern United States that have experienced directly most wars fought on United States soil. Williamsburg was a battle scene during the Revolutionary War (discussed in chapter five), the War of 1812, and the Civil War—with the exception of Indian wars, the only three wars fought on U.S. soil. During the Revolutionary War, the city experienced much of Cornwallis's 1781 invasion of Virginia and its culmination in the Battle of Yorktown.

The British also invaded the peninsula in the War of 1812. After burning Hampton at the start of the war, the British and Americans skirmished amid a British landing on the peninsula in early summer 1813, plus a second British landing later that summer on Jamestown Island (a raiding party bent on seizing booty). From then until the end of the war in December 1814, Williamsburg citizens worried that British troops might quickly return to the peninsula. The British enjoyed naval superiority as the Napoleonic wars ended in Europe, and they could dispatch units of their huge fleet to the United States. The British army had substantial training and far more experience than did the American army of the time. The United States was lucky to escape as lightly scathed as she was by the war. Although the British did damage to the peninsula (including the burning of Hampton) and, especially, the James River shoreline houses and plantations, the city itself was largely spared.

Parke Rouse relates one of the more interesting stories from Williamsburg during the War of 1812. Commodore Lewis L. Warrington, a hero of the war, was born the illegitimate son of a French officer and Williamsburg girl in 1782, shortly after the

After 1783: Between the Revolution and Civil War

Battle of Yorktown. The story goes that Mrs. Susanna Riddell moved into the Brush-Everard house with two female wards, Camilla and Rachel Warrington. Rachel gave birth on November 3, 1782, to a boy she called Lewis Warrington. Rouse saw unpublished Elizabeth Ambler letters that name Joseph Rochambeau, General Rochambeau's thirty-one-year-old son, as the father. How she met the younger Rochambeau is unclear, although it may have been when she was working hospital duty and he was a patient after the campaign. When the war officially ended, he went back to France and did not acknowledge his son. Rachel married Richard Brown of York County in 1786.

When Lewis Warrington grew up, he joined the United States Navy as a midshipman at the age of eighteen. He rose in rank to command the *Peacock* in the War of 1812. His ship met and defeated the British ship *Epervier*, winning him a medal from Congress. Eventually he reached the rank of commodore, the Navy's highest in the early nineteenth century. When Lewis's father heard in France of his son's accomplishments, he wrote him and offered to legitimize him. The son rejected the offer. He died in 1851, still serving in the Navy.

After 1815, Virginia and the peninsula still were economically sluggish. Soils exhausted by over a century-and-a-half of tobacco growing, a legislature dominated by conservative Tidewater planters, and a population rapidly moving west contributed to economic stagnation. The city and state also felt the sting of the nation's first financial panic (1819) and subsequent depression. But in Virginia there were those seeking to improve the state's economic outlook. In Loudoun County in the early nineteenth century some farmers began to use modern techniques of soil enrichment, adding marl and other fertilizers, plus using new crop rotations and methods of plowing to enrich the soil and make it more friable. Others encouraged economic development, particularly transportation improvements to move passengers and freight more quickly and to more different locations. Canal construction, road building, and, later in the 1830s, railroad creation in Virginia suggest the interest many Virginia entrepreneurs had in improving the state's economy. But the peninsula lagged in developing adequate transportation to move people and goods to the west and south. The bay and rivers provided good water transportation eastward and northward, but peninsula entrepreneurs neglected westerly and southerly directions until much later in the nineteenth century. The state created a board of public works to aid localities in planning and building transportation improvements and systems, but Williamsburg benefited little from the project. In 1818 a plan was put forward for construction of a canal linking the city with College Creek. The canal's path was surveyed, but nothing ever came of the plan. Observers described roads as wagon paths and likened the city's streets to pastures, complete with domestic animals of all sorts grazing in them.

Peninsula watermen fished, crabbed, and tonged for oysters during the appropriate seasons; Williamsburg residents enjoyed the bounties of those fin and shellfish as they did other delicacies of the palate, and as had been done in the former capital's heyday. But the city continued its rural and, as many nineteenth-century residents put it, sleepy existence. There were times besides the 1807 bicentennial of the settlement of Jamestown and War of 1812 when the city came to life. One of those times was the 1824 visit of the Marquis de Lafayette. Invited by Congress as the "Nation's Guest" for the year, the Marquis, Marie Joseph Paul Yves Roch Gilbert du Motier, arrived in the area on October 19, 1824, the forty-third anniversary of Cornwallis's surrender of the British army. He stayed in Yorktown that day and evening, but then went to Williamsburg where he made an address (one of many he made that year throughout the young country) in which he reminisced on the significance of the city and the college during the colonial and revolutionary eras.

He was especially complimentary of the college, which he called "the parent of so many enlightened patriots who have illustrated the Virginia name." His reminiscences spoke of the many Virginians he had known at the time of the Revolution and praised the "generous minds whose early resolutions came forth in support of their heroic Boston brethren." Hostesses in the city vied with each other to get Lafayette to stay at their house; the winner was Mrs. Mary Monroe Peachy, whose house had during the siege of Yorktown in 1781 been General Rochambeau's headquarters. He stayed at the house, known as the Peyton Randolph house, until October 21 when he left Williamsburg.

Although Lafayette was well entertained in the city, those of his party who left impressions of the town thought it small and ramshackle. One of Lafayette's aides remarked that the town was decaying and its population declining. Other visitors about the same time remarked similarly, calling it a "paltry village," trading on its earlier glory. The city did have some life in the antebellum era, a life marked by its status as the county seat for James City County, the hospital, the college, and its value as a market town.

In the eyes of one of the city's historians, town life in the 1820s centered around the combination general store and post office. One could find books, hams, brandy, silk stockings, mail, chewing tobacco, and medicines, just to suggest the diversity of the shop. Men gathered there to dicuss everything from presidential elections to the quality of Irish potatoes (potatoes were domesticated in the South American Andes by Native Americans and then transported to the rest of the world after Pizarro's conquest of the Incan Empire in the 1530s). By contrast, Williamsburg in the 1760s had been an imperial capital, important in European and North American affairs.

In the antebellum era many residents could not afford to maintain their homes and keep them in repair, so the houses and outbuildings deteriorated in the hot, humid Tidewater summers and cold, rainy, snowy Tidewater winters. Adding to the climate problems was a tornado that touched down on June 21, 1834, in James City County and Williamsburg. Two men died when the building in which they sought shelter fell on them. The city experienced fallen trees and collapsed chimneys, although there were apparently no other deaths. The tornado crossed York County and the York River into Gloucester County as well, continuing its path of destruction.

If residents experienced various levels of impoverishment, so too did the city's hinterland, the region from which Williamsburgers derived their food and other resources. Rural life in nineteenth-century peninsula Virginia was also beset with problems of poverty and, particularly, land degradation. Tobacco takes a heavy toll on thin, sandy agricultural soils, the types most prevalent in the Tidewater region. By 1800 many farming families were either giving up their agricultural ways or, if they still had money, moving west to regions of the new nation where there were more fertile lands. Although some planters in the area still grew tobacco, many others who kept at their farming elected to try other crops, ones that would produce some profitable returns. These included wheat and corn, vegetables, and some fruits. Orchards had been an important part of Tidewater farms and plantations since the seventeenth century, but the orchards' fruits had usually been turned into some form of alcoholic drink, brandy or jack, for consumption on the farm or plantation itself. But after the Revolution some Tidewater farmers began selling dried or fresh fruit, yet whatever they tried to do in the decades between the Revolution and Civil War, it was not enough. The economy remained stalled and underdeveloped.

As the decades passed, however, some economic change began in the city and peninsula. Agricultural change, begun earlier in the nineteenth century, revived in the aftermath of the Panic and Depression of 1837. In the 1840s local farmers began to improve their lands through additions of marl and lime both to sweeten the soil (made increasingly acidic by overuse and tobacco production) and loosen it up to make it more friable. By the 1840s a number of technological changes in agriculture such as improved plows, reapers, mowers, seeders, and threshing machines made farming not only easier but more productive. New crops, or varieties of crops, increased yields per acre. Peninsula farmers began planting potatoes, both white and sweet, for commercial crops. They joined agricultural societies, read agricultural journals, and some wrote articles for journals and magazines. Agricultural fairs became popular in the mid-nineteenth century and they encouraged competition in the production of prize crops and animals. In 1854, farmers in the Williamsburg area organized an agricultural society that held fairs and competitions.

Most rural and urban work was performed by slaves. Over 50 percent of James City County's population (including Williamsburg) was enslaved in the mid-nineteenth century. There was an increasing number of free blacks and mulattoes, however, a population that suggests some sort of dramatic social change occurring in the region in the twenty years before the Civil War. Agricultural technology lessened the need for rural slaves, but an increase in mulattoes indicates a rising number of white and black unions. Such unions were illegal, but federal censuses indicate substantial growth in mixed-race populations between 1830 and 1860.

Slaves still did the vast majority of plantation work, planting, and harvesting the tobacco, wheat, corn, potatoes, fruits, vegetables, and other commodities grown on peninsula plantations. Urban slaves still, as in the colonial era, did most of the hard work in the city. Slaves' values, however, had appreciated considerably since the Revolution and Virginia became a major source of slaves in the nineteenth century. Declining tobacco prices meant reduced tobacco production; the lack of a substitute commercial staple crop (as short-staple cotton became in the lower south after 1800), the unwillingness of rural planters to convert their slaves into industrial workers, and a growing slave population presented planters with the option of selling their slaves in large numbers "Down South." During the 1830s, 1840s, and 1850s slave traders from the deep south (South Carolina, Georgia, Florida, Alabama, Mississippi, Louisiana, and Texas) bought in Virginia sizeable numbers of slaves whom they formed into coffles of 200 to 300 linked together by chains and manacles, and walked them to the lower south where they were sold for sizeable profits.

The acquisition of new territory in the 1840s (Texas, the Mexican Cession, Oregon) added about one third of the current landmass of the "Lower 48" to the Union. Southern slaveholders considered much of that territory suitable for slavery and they wanted to move their families to new, fresh lands on which to grow cotton or other staple crops. Virginia, Maryland, Kentucky, and other Upper South states, all having large numbers of slaves, sold their "surplus" slaves into the lower south. Although James City County's slave population remained about 50 percent of the county's total population, that number did not grow during the quarter century before the Civil War; it remained the same. Although death took many, slave sales south were often brisk during the antebellum era.

The issue of slavery began to tear apart the nation during the three decades before 1860. European nations with colonial empires in the Americas began abolishing slavery within their imperial domains in the 1790s (when Revolutionary

Continued on page 97

John Smith's "Map of Virginia" shows Indian villages his reconnoitering parties charted during their explorations of the Chesapeake Bay in 1607–1608. North is to the right. (Courtesy Visual Resources Center, John D. Rockefeller Library, Colonial Williamsburg, Inc.)

An Indian werowance, or leader, from De Bry derived from a White watercolor. White's watercolor shows the native's tattoos, clothing, weapons, and symbols of authority. Verbal descriptions of Virginia Indian leaders reflect this visual depiction. (Courtesy Visual Resources Center, John D. Rockefeller Library, Colonial Williamsburg, Inc.)

Prehistoric Indian hearth (lower center), consisting of fire-cracked rocks and pottery fragments. Located on the outskirts of Williamsburg, the hearth lies about two feet below current grade and rests within a structure dating to 660 A.D., ±forty years. (Courtesy Alain C. Outlaw, Archaeological & Cultural Solutions, Inc., Williamsburg.)

A conjectural view of Jamestown in the early 1620s. The view, known as Mrs. Dayton's, shows how the town had spread eastward from its waterfront fort c.1607. Some buildings were made of brick. (Courtesy Visual Resources Center, John D. Rockefeller Library, Colonial Williamsburg, Inc.)

A conjectural representation of the many ways Indians attacked whites in the March 1622 assault on the English colony. Note the rather elaborate, but fanciful fort, firing large cannon in the background. (Courtesy Visual Resources Center, John D. Rockefeller Library, Colonial Williamsburg, Inc.)

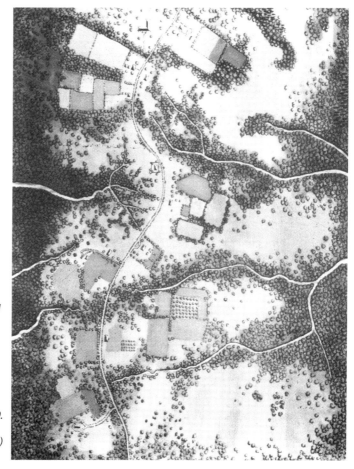

A conjectural aerial view of Middle Plantation, showing the winding road running through the settlement. Note the number of ravines and small streams leading north to the York River and south to the James. (Courtesy Visual Resources Center, John D. Rockefeller Library, Colonial Williamsburg, Inc.)

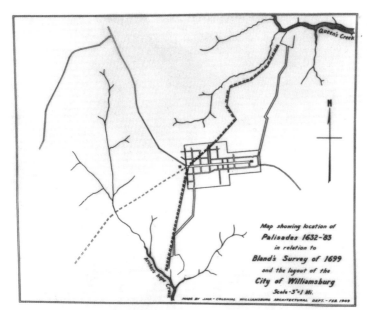

A Colonial Williamsburg Architectural Department's representation of the layout of the palisade's path as it was constructed in the 1620s and later. The palisade is shown in relation to the later formal survey and layout of the City of Williamsburg itself. (Courtesy Visual Resources Center, John D. Rockefeller Library, Colonial Williamsburg, Inc.)

An artist's rendition of Bruton Parish Church with planters and their families gathered along the roadway beside it. The church became a religious and cultural center for the colony and city. (Courtesy Visual Resources Center, John D. Rockefeller Library, Colonial Williamsburg, Inc.)

A survey of the general outline of the town, plus the roads to the two small ports, done by Theodorick Bland in 1698. The survey shows how Bland and Nicholson used town planning techniques to design the city's boundaries. (Courtesy Visual Resources Center, John D. Rockefeller Library, Colonial Williamsburg, Inc.)

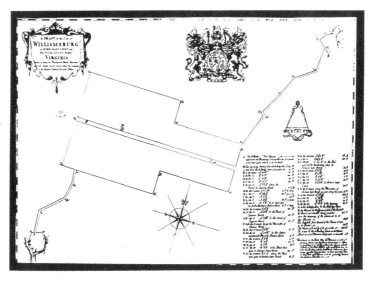

A toneline drawing of the Capitol, the first public building erected in the city after its creation. The drawing shows the symmetry and order of the building. (Courtesy Visual Resources Center, John D. Rockefeller Library, Colonial Williamsburg, Inc.)

A photograph of a painting of the Governor's Palace shortly after its reconstruction. The painting, done in 1936, shows the building and glimpses of the two buildings flanking the entrance. (Courtesy Visual Resources Center, John D. Rockefeller Library, Colonial Williamsburg, Inc.)

An illustration of a tobacco plant, the plant that launched Virginia's landed population into substantial wealth. The central plant, Nicotiana Tabaccum, is the one most used by Chesapeake Bay tobacco planters in the seventeenth and eighteenth centuries. (Courtesy Visual Resources Center, John D. Rockefeller Library, Colonial Williamsburg, Inc.)

A detail of the cartouche on the Frye-Jefferson Map of 1751, this illustration shows how planters, watermen, slaves, and seamen participated in the Chesapeake Bay's tobacco trade. Note the large barrels (presumably hogsheads of tobacco) and the tobacco ships in the background that will carry the "weed" to markets in England and the rest of Europe. (Courtesy Visual Resources Center, John D. Rockefeller Library, Colonial Williamsburg, Inc.)

This plate, known as the Bodleian Plate, was found in the 1920s in England. It, along with the Frenchman's Map, provided invaluable information about how the College, Capitol, and Palace looked in the mid-eighteenth century. (Courtesy Visual Resources Center, John D. Rockefeller Library, Colonial Williamsburg, Inc.)

Although Williamsburg had its own domestic, urban economy, it still relied heavily on rural tobacco production and sale. This composite shows tobacco processing and preparing for market. (Courtesy Visual Resources Center, John D. Rockefeller Library, Colonial Williamsburg, Inc.)

George III (reigned 1760–1820) in his coronation robes for his coronation painting. Very popular with Virginia colonials at the start of his reign, King George became a symbol of authoritarianism by the mid-1770s. (Courtesy Visual Resources Center, John D. Rockefeller Library, Colonial Williamsburg, Inc.)

Lieutenant Governor Alexander Spotswood, who sat as governor from 1710–1722. He was responsible for designing many of the public buildings, especially the Palace, as it came to be called. (Courtesy Visual Resources Center, John D. Rockefeller Library, Colonial Williamsburg, Inc.)

Governor Francis Fauquier, who served in Virginia in the 1760s. A popular governor, he was partly responsible for maintaining good relations between the colony and England. (Courtesy Visual Resources Center, John D. Rockefeller Library, Colonial Williamsburg, Inc.)

Lord Dunmore, the last royal governor of Virginia. Virginians regarded him ambiguously until the crucial year 1775–1776. This detail from a miniature shows him in old age, years after his governorship of the colony. (Courtesy Visual Resources Center, John D. Rockefeller Library, Colonial Williamsburg, Inc.)

Lord Botetourt, one of Virginia's more popular late-colonial governors. He died very soon after assuming office and Virginians in memoriam had a statue of him made for the college, where it still resides. (Courtesy Visual Resources Center, John D. Rockefeller Library, Colonial Williamsburg, Inc.)

A view of the Raleigh Tavern taken from Benson Lossing's nineteeth-century work, showing the exterior of the building where many plans for revolution were carried out in the name of liberty, yet at the same time, slaves were frequently sold from an auction block in the front. Below: The Apollo Room of the Raleigh, where many Patriots gathered during the crisis years to discuss courses of action against England. (Courtesy Visual Resources Center, John D. Rockefeller Library, Colonial Williamsburg, Inc.)

This etching, titled "The Alternative of Williams Burg," was published in England as a depiction of Williamsburgers' resistance to British policy. (Courtesy Visual Resources Center, John D. Rockefeller Library, Colonial Williamsburg, Inc.)

This view of the old Capitol building shows it after its reconstruction following the 1747 fire. (Courtesy Visual Resources Center, John D. Rockefeller Library, Colonial Williamsburg, Inc.)

A toneline drawing of Wetherburn's Tavern, made during its reconstruction and restoration. The tavern was a very popular socializing spot in the colonial-era city. (Courtesy Visual Resources Center, John D. Rockefeller Library, Colonial Williamsburg, Inc.)

The crucial phase of the Siege of Yorktown was made possible by the little-known Battle of the Capes on September 5, 1781, when a French fleet successfully defeated a British fleet, just off the Virginia Capes. This French success gave the Franco-American allies control of Virginia's waters, enabling the allied land armies to entrap Cornwallis at Yorktown. (Courtesy Visual Resources Center, John D. Rockefeller Library, Colonial Williamsburg, Inc.)

Washington and his generals at Yorktown. (Courtesy Visual Resources Center, John D. Rockefeller Library, Colonial Williamsburg, Inc.)

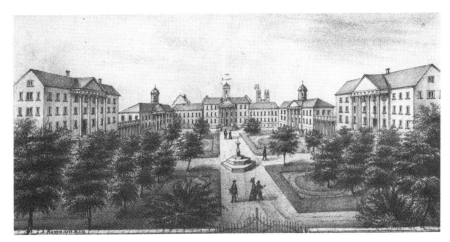

The Public Hospital, renamed the Eastern Lunatic Asylum in the nineteenth century, as it existed in the 1850s in Williamsburg. (Courtesy Visual Resources Center, John D. Rockefeller Library, Colonial Williamsburg, Inc.)

The Main, or Wren Building at the College of William and Mary shortly after it burned in 1859 (above), and right after its reconstruction (below), showing the Italianate influences with the two bell towers at the front of the building. (Courtesy Visual Resources Center, John D. Rockefeller Library, Colonial Williamsburg, Inc.)

One of the first photographs of Williamsburg, taken from the second story of the Wren Building in 1859 (probably just before the fire), looking east on Duke of Gloucester Street during winter. The Williamsburg Female Seminary can barely be made out at the other end of the street, but Bruton Parish Church is clearly visible. (Courtesy Visual Resources Center, John D. Rockefeller Library, Colonial Williamsburg, Inc.)

Constructed in the early 1850s, the Williamsburg Female Seminary sat on the site of the colonial Capitol building at the east end of Duke of Gloucester Street. (Courtesy Visual Resources Center, John D. Rockefeller Library, Colonial Williamsburg, Inc.)

THE HOSPITAL ON THE BATTLEFIELD OF WILLIAMSBURG.—UNION AND CONFEDERATE SURGEONS ATTENDING.—Sketched by Private Fortescue.

An engraving showing a field hospital at the Battle of Williamsburg in Spring 1862. Much of the town was a hospital during the battle. (Courtesy Visual Resources Center, John D. Rockefeller Library, Colonial Williamsburg, Inc.)

THE BATTLE OF WILLIAMSBURG, VA., ON THE PENINSULA BETWEEN YORK AND JAMES RIVERS, MAY 6, 1852.—Sketched by A. Waud.

An engraving depicting a portion of the Battle of Williamsburg on May 5, 1862. The battle delayed Union General George McClellan's advance up the peninsula toward Richmond enough to allow Confederate forces plenty of time to prepare their defenses. (Courtesy Visual Resources Center, John D. Rockefeller Library, Colonial Williamsburg, Inc.)

An oxcart with a black driver (recently freed from slavery by the Civil War and Thirteenth Amendment to the Constitution) driving along Duke of Gloucester Street in front of the Baptist Church with the Williamsburg Hotel to the right and the magazine to the rear. (Courtesy Visual Resources Center, John D. Rockefeller Library, Colonial Williamsburg, Inc.)

Williamsburg remained a small, southern country town during the late nineteenth century, as evidenced by the two chickens scratching for food in the dust of Duke of Gloucester Street. (Courtesy Visual Resources Center, John D. Rockefeller Library, Colonial Williamsburg, Inc.)

An elderly black man walking past the 1770 Courthouse on the north side of Duke of Gloucester Street in the late nineteenth century, probably late in fall. (Courtesy Visual Resources Center, John D. Rockefeller Library, Colonial Williamsburg, Inc.)

A mother and children on Duke of Gloucester Street in the late nineteenth century. The Ludwell-Paradise House (the two-story brick building at right center) was the first building acquired for the restoration. (Courtesy Visual Resources Center, John D. Rockefeller Library, Colonial Williamsburg, Inc.)

Residents gathering to shop at Samuel Harris's Cheap Store on Duke of Gloucester Street in the late nineteenth century. Note the large number of oxcarts as opposed to horse-drawn vehicles on the street. (Courtesy Visual Resources Center, John D. Rockefeller Library, Colonial Williamsburg, Inc.)

A pre-1905 view of Bruton Parish Church (before its restoration) showing Williamsburg as a quiet, sleepy, small town. (Courtesy Visual Resources Center, John D. Rockefeller Library, Colonial Williamsburg, Inc.)

A portion of the city's business section, the south side of Duke of Gloucester Street, in the early twentieth century, looking south across Courthouse Green, post–World War I. (Courtesy Visual Resources Center, John D. Rockefeller Library, Colonial Williamsburg, Inc.)

Three views of Duke of Gloucester Street.

Top: pre–World War I before paving and the median with power/phone poles. Today the area is part of Merchants' Square.

Middle: fall or winter 1928 showing the median and power/phone poles, a tire store, and 1920s-vintage automobiles.

Bottom: c.1930, showing a Baptist Church to the immediate right. Three years later the median and poles disappeared as all utilities were placed underground during the restoration.

(Courtesy Visual Resources Center, John D. Rockefeller Library, Colonial Williamsburg, Inc.)

The principal and students in the auditorium of the James City County Training School in the late 1920s. (Courtesy Visual Resources Center, John D. Rockefeller Library, Colonial Williamsburg, Inc.)

The new and the old—an ox-drawn carriage passes a parked auto in front of the Bruton Parish Church wall on Duke of Gloucester Street in the late 1920s. (Courtesy Visual Resources Center, John D. Rockefeller Library, Colonial Williamsburg, Inc.)

Peyton Randolph Nelson, a "town character" with his long beard, herding his cows in town. Descended from two prominent Virginia families, the Randolphs and Nelsons, he lived in the city for several decades during the early twentieth century. (Courtesy Visual Resources Center, John D. Rockefeller Library, Colonial Williamsburg, Inc.)

During the restoration the town was literally torn up, especially Duke of Gloucester Street. This photo shows construction of the tunnel that carries the Colonial Parkway under the restoration, looking south from Courthouse Green with the Courthouse of 1770 to the west. (Courtesy Visual Resources Center, John D. Rockefeller Library, Colonial Williamsburg, Inc.)

The Reverend W.A.R. Goodwin, Episcopal minister and teacher, was responsible for convincing John D. Rockefeller Jr. of the need to finance the restoration of Williamsburg to its colonial past. Goodwin remained active in the town from his return in the early 1920s until his death. (Courtesy Visual Resources Center, John D. Rockefeller Library, Colonial Williamsburg, Inc.)

John D. Rockefeller Jr. was the man responsible for financing Williamsburg's restoration beginning in the 1920s. Rockefeller was heir to one of the largest fortunes in the nation, built on his father's Standard Oil profits. Using his inherited wealth, Rockefeller provided the monies and much of the direction to the early period of the restoration. (Courtesy Visual Resources Center, John D. Rockefeller Library, Colonial Williamsburg, Inc.)

An archaeological photo taken of the excavated foundations of the Capitol building in the late 1920s and early 1930s, one of the first buildings reconstructed in the restoration. (Courtesy Visual Resources Center, John D. Rockefeller Library, Colonial Williamsburg, Inc.)

Virginia Governor John Pollard (a Williamsburg resident) addresses the crowd at the formal opening of the Raleigh Tavern in the early 1930s. (Courtesy Visual Resources Center, John D. Rockefeller Library, Colonial Williamsburg, Inc.)

This photo is a view from the recently-completed Capitol building looking west up Duke of Gloucester Street. President Franklin D. Roosevelt (seated in the back of the touring car) arrived to tour the restoration and give a speech honoring the idea. (Courtesy Visual Resources Center, John D. Rockefeller Library, Colonial Williamsburg, Inc.)

The USO club in Williamsburg formally opened in 1943 with John D. Rockefeller Jr., his wife Abby Aldrich Rockefeller, and three service men attending. Rockefeller wanted a USO club in the city to provide service men and women entertainment as well as edification when they came to tour the restoration. (Courtesy Visual Resources Center, John D. Rockefeller Library, Colonial Williamsburg, Inc.)

In the 1950s many of Williamsburg's services such as fire protection retained their volunteer status. The Williamsburg Fire Department in 1957 reflected the commitment of many men to their community. (Courtesy Visual Resources Center, John D. Rockefeller Library, Colonial Williamsburg, Inc.)

To encourage cooperation between the restoration and townspeople, Colonial Williamsburg put on ceremonies reminiscent of eighteenth-century social events. Here the townspeople, guests of the restoration, and costumed Colonial Williamsburg employees enjoy the 1953 annual Yule Log Ceremony. (Courtesy Visual Resources Center, John D. Rockefeller Library, Colonial Williamsburg, Inc.)

In 1957 Jamestown commemorated its 350th anniversary and Queen Elizabeth II and her Royal Consort Prince Philip visited the reconstructed village. Courtesy: (Courtesy Visual Resources Center, John D. Rockefeller Library, Colonial Williamsburg, Inc.)

African Americans in a segregated society relaxed and enjoyed themselves at places like Yorkie's Tavern in James City County during the 1950s. This photograph was taken by Albert Durant, a local African-American chauffeur. Durant's photographic collection, now housed at the Rockefeller Library, is a powerful statement about black life in Williamsburg and surrounding areas during the 1930s, 1940s, and 1950s. (Courtesy Visual Resources Center, John D. Rockefeller Library, Colonial Williamsburg, Inc.)

Albert Durant took many photos of blacks in social settings. Williamsburg and James City County blacks gathered at Log Cabin Beach on the James River, a segregated beach with picnic facilities. (Courtesy Visual Resources Center, John D. Rockefeller Library, Colonial Williamsburg, Inc.)

Another Durant photograph, this one shows a group of African-American hunters having killed a stag in the late 1940s. (Courtesy Visual Resources Center, John D. Rockefeller Library, Colonial Williamsburg, Inc.)

African Americans who chose to join one of the local Baptist churches in Williamsburg or the surrounding area were baptized en masse in the James River, as shown by another of Durant's photos. (Courtesy Visual Resources Center, John D. Rockefeller Library, Colonial Williamsburg, Inc.)

The Reverend Lardrew Johnson, one of the leaders of the Williamsburg African-American community, celebrates Christmas with his family in the 1950s. Reverend Johnson was pastor of First Baptist Church in the city and Albert Durant photographed his family and him. (Courtesy Visual Resources Center, John D. Rockefeller Library, Colonial Williamsburg, Inc.)

Symbolic of the growing partnership between the city and the restoration after World War II, this photo shows Colonial Williamsburg Foundation's Kenneth Chorley and Williamsburg Mayor Henry M. "Polly" Stryker. (Courtesy Visual Resources Center, John D. Rockefeller Library, Colonial Williamsburg, Inc.)

The College of William and Mary, the City of Williamsburg, and Colonial Williamsburg join in 1998 to welcome incoming freshmen to the college. (Courtesy Visual Resources Center, John D. Rockefeller Library, Colonial Williamsburg, Inc.)

Albert Durant also photographed non–African American local scenes, such as this groundbreaking for Anheuser-Busch's brewery in the late 1960s. (Courtesy Visual Resources Center, John D. Rockefeller Library, Colonial Williamsburg, Inc.)

The American Revolution bicentennial was a major event in Williamsburg in 1976. Here the Fife and Drum Corps entertain visitors and townspeople outside the Lodge in 1975. (Courtesy Visual Resources Center, John D. Rockefeller Library, Colonial Williamsburg, Inc.)

The city, college, and Colonial Williamsburg joined together during the bicentennial to present a series of lectures and panels on the meaning of independence, usually in the Capitol building, such as this session. (Courtesy Visual Resources Center, John D. Rockefeller Library, Colonial Williamsburg, Inc.)

The site of First Baptist Church was dedicated with a memorial plaque; congregants moved the church to its present site in 1955. (Courtesy Visual Resources Center, John D. Rockefeller Library, Colonial Williamsburg, Inc.)

The Colonial Militia salutes the Fourth of July in 1983 with a volley from its cannon. These occasions provide townspeople and tourists alike the opportunity to experience some of the noise and smells of eighteenth-century warfare. (Courtesy Visual Resources Center, John D. Rockefeller Library, Colonial Williamsburg, Inc.)

A 1989 version of "Publick Times" shows that merchandising of Colonial Williamsburg's wares continues to be a healthy enterprise. (Courtesy Visual Resources Center, John D. Rockefeller Library, Colonial Williamsburg, Inc.)

In the last few decades, Colonial Williamsburg has sponsored breakfasts for community leaders (such as this one in 2001) to provide opportunities for leaders to gather and discuss ideas about the city and foundation. (Courtesy Visual Resources Center, John D. Rockefeller Library, Colonial Williamsburg, Inc.)

After 1783: Between the Revolution and Civil War

Continued from page 64

France ended slavery in her American empire). Great Britain followed suit in the 1830s. As former Spanish colonies like Mexico became independent, they too abolished the institution. By 1860 American slavery legally existed only in Brazil, the United States, and what remained of Spain's American empire (Caribbean islands like Cuba). The British tried to end the international slave trade, also. They sought to interdict slavers at the African coast, and the United States entered its Navy in the blockade, too. But slave smugglers continued to bring Africans illegally to the United States, and many were smuggled to the peninsula, although there was a surplus of slaves in the area.

With the acquisition of substantial new amounts of territory between 1845 and 1848, competition between slave and free states for access to those territories became fierce. The issue of slavery entwined itself into almost every political, religious, and cultural question of the United States by 1860. But one of the most important questions was the disposition of the "peculiar institution" (Southern politicians' euphemism for slavery) in the newly-acquired territories. Would slaveholders be permitted by law to take their slaves into the Great Plains, the Rocky Mountains, Oregon, California, and all the other lands? In seeking answers to this question, politicians (whose abilities and characters had slipped considerably below those of earlier generations) offered many compromises and remedies, but none suited. Either Southern or Northern political opinion revolted at solutions offered. If Northerners approved of a solution, Southerners did not and vice versa.

Williamsburg residents generally supported slavery and the arguments associated to protect slavery in the Union. Some residents, even prominent ones, did not, so just as other areas of the nation bitterly divided over the issue of slavery so did Williamsburg. One of the city's own, John Tyler, had much to do with bringing on the crisis. Tyler, born in Charles City County, became President when William Henry Harrison died about one month after his inauguration in 1841. During his presidency his first wife Letitia died and he soon remarried to a much younger woman, Julia, with whom he had a second family of seven children.

Before his elevation to the presidency, Tyler lived in Williamsburg on Francis Street, in a house built for Robert Carter Nicholas during the colonial era. The house, large and roomy, provided ample space for Tyler and his first family. As his presidency neared its end, however, he sold the house in order to buy Sherwood Forest, a house just across the James City County line in Charles City County, which he occupied with his second family until his death in 1862. The Williamsburg house, however, burned to the ground in the 1870s and a new James City County courthouse was built on the site during the restoration in the 1930s.

Williamsburg

Tyler, an apostate Democrat, affiliated with the Whig political party because he despised Andrew Jackson and believed Jackson had grossly overstepped his authority while President. But Tyler did not share many Whig policies or much of the Whig ideology. When he began to move toward his version of Democratic policies, his whole cabinet resigned. He appointed new men who generally agreed with what he wanted to do. Most importantly from the standpoint of disunity, Tyler wanted very much to acquire new territory, especially Texas because it would expand slave territory. When ardent expansionist James Knox Polk eked out a narrow victory in the 1844 election, Tyler eagerly sought Polk's aid in securing Texas's admission (an independent republic at the time) to the Union. Between the fall 1844 election and Polk's inauguration in March 1845, such did happen. Tyler returned to Virginia satisfied he had done much to advance the interests of the nation without violating either his strict constructionist principles on the Constitution or his commitment to states' rights. Instead, one of the most unpopular wars in the nation's history broke out between Mexico and the United States.

Polk deliberately provoked Mexico into firing the first shots, but he waged the war to annex even more territory, known as the Mexican Cession. In the free states there was widespread reaction, including burning of the Constitution and flag, in opposition to the war. Many reasons account for the opposition, but the most important was the acquisition of new slave territory. It was during this war that Henry David Thoreau refused to pay his taxes, saying he would not pay for a war to expand slavery.

It was in this stew of emotions and insecurities that the Civil War began. Williamsburg, a sleepy, slow, rural community in the mid-nineteenth century, became, due to the vagaries of preparations for and conduct of war, a centerpiece in the fighting of the Civil War. The peninsula, because of geography of land and water, was a major staging point for the war.

Chapter Six

WILLIAMSBURG
AND THE CIVIL WAR ERA

During the 1850s the United States divided over the issue of slavery and its introduction into new territories acquired in the mid-1840s. Northern and Southern politicians bitterly denounced each other's section and Southern politicians repeatedly threatened secession if abolitionists did not stop threatening their "peculiar institution." Although politicians tried compromises such as the Compromise of 1850 or the Kansas-Nebraska Act, they ultimately did little good. The formation of the Republican Party between 1854 and 1856 and its dedication to keeping slavery confined to the fifteen states in which it existed at the time frustrated Democrats and Southerners alike who wished to see the institution pushed into the new territories.

Williamsburg citizens generally regarded the question of secession as a legal and constitutional solution to the problems dividing the nation at the time. When, after Abraham Lincoln's election to the presidency in 1860, seven deep south states (South Carolina, Georgia, Florida, Alabama, Mississippi, Louisiana, and Texas) declared themselves out of the Union and formed a new nation called the Confederate States of America dedicated to the preservation of slavery, Williamsburg citizens generally accepted that decision. When residents of Charleston, South Carolina, fired on Fort Sumter, the last Federal-retained piece of property in South Carolina, Virginia, including a majority of Williamsburg citizens, voted to leave the Union and join the Confederacy.

When Virginia seceded from the Union in April 1861, almost every able-bodied man in Williamsburg immediately volunteered for the Confederate Army. All the students, faculty, and even the president of William and Mary joined the rebel army, closing the college for the war's duration. The peninsula, however, had a large Union military presence in Fort Monroe, located at the entrance to Hampton Roads near the town of Hampton. From there, Union armies embarked on a campaign to besiege and conquer Richmond, the city to which the Confederate government moved its capital after Virginia's secession.

The peninsula, strategically important to both Union and Confederate forces, had its share of intrigue, warfare, and destruction during the war, but it also drew large numbers of slaves who fled their plantations when they heard of the Union Army's presence at Fort Monroe. In summer 1861, three slaves made their way to Fort Monroe from the environs of the town of Hampton. They requested their freedom. General Benjamin Butler, commanding Union forces then, faced a dilemma. The slaves' master demanded their return as fugitive slaves. Butler, who thought slavery ought to end in the nation at that time, made a momentous decision. He told the slaves' master that since Virginia had seceded, the 1850 Fugitive Slave Act no longer applied in the state and, moreover, the slaves, who could easily be used as labor to aid Confederate Army endeavors to defeat Union forces, were, by the then-existing laws of war, contraband of war. Butler skillfully used the Confederacy's own definitions of slaves as chattel property to make and enforce his decision. From that time, escaped slaves who made their way to Union lines were called contraband. During the rest of the war, the numbers of contrabands on the lower peninsula swelled to thousands as Virginia, northeastern North Carolina, and other Southern slaves made their way to the peninsula to seek shelter with the occupying Union forces.

Fort Monroe remained a Union stronghold in Confederate Virgina during the whole war. Union war strategy called for a large offensive operation to divide the Confederacy along the Mississippi River, and then redivide it southeastward through the Southern states while at the same time maintaining constant pressure on the Confederate capital at Richmond. Fort Monroe remained a staging base for that latter prong of Union strategy.

When William and Mary College president Benjamin Ewell resigned in 1861 to volunteer for Confederate forces, he was soon assigned to develop defenses for the city against Union forces at Fort Monroe. Using slaves and free blacks as labor, he directed construction of earthworks east of the city to protect both the city and the peninsular approaches to Richmond. Joined by units from as far away as Georgia and Louisiana, Confederate forces soon built earthworks across the peninsula just east of the city. Then in August 1861, the Confederate general commanding the peninsula's defenses, John Bankhead Magruder, ordered Hampton burned to prevent its falling to Union troops from Fort Monroe. Williamsburg residents soon began fearing a similar fate for their town and rumors of imminent destruction of the town by Confederate forces circulated from then until the Battle of Williamsburg in May 1862.

In the meantime, the town became a hospital. High levels of illness, mostly typhoid fever that sprang up seasonally (mid to late summer), brought many rebel troops to bed for prolonged periods. Those who maintained their health were prone to destruction and vandalism. Taking wood from fences and house siding, breaking into houses temporarily abandoned by Confederates gone to other parts of the

Confederacy, or even just raising rumors of burning the town, Confederate troops occupying the town raised apprehensions and fears. But during the whole first year of the war, rumors of imminent Union invasion of the peninsula abounded.

Finally, those rumors of Union approach came true when Union General George McClellan decided to begin his "On to Richmond" campaign in early 1862. He directed the deployment of the Union Army of the Potomac to Fort Monroe. In late winter and early spring 1862 over 100,000 Union army officers and men journeyed from the Washington, D.C. area to Fort Monroe. There they encamped awaiting McClellan's decision on when to undertake the offensive. In the meantime, Confederate forces under Magruder built more defensive works across the peninsula from Yorktown to the James River, running just east of the city. Magruder and his forces numbered only a few thousand, but he used many subterfuges to convince the overly-cautious McClellan that he had almost as many men as McClellan. The various strategems worked, causing McClellan to delay while Confederate Commanding General Joseph Johnston moved down the peninsula from northern Virginia to reinforce Magruder.

After many skirmishes and encounters, on May 5, 1862, Union and Confederate forces fought the Battle of Williamsburg with Confederate forces retreating to Richmond in heavy rain. Many Williamsburg residents went to the battlefield, with umbrellas, to watch the fight between the two forces; they returned to their homes frightened and upset as Union forces settled into the town. McClellan characteristically did not pursue, leaving Confederate armies in good shape to complete the defense of Richmond. Union forces now occupied Williamsburg for the rest of the war, with the exception of one day. The Prince de Joinville, one of a small group of French observers living with Union forces, commented about the battle and entry into Williamsburg:

> The rains began to fall in torrents and poured down incessantly for thirty consecutive hours. The country became one vast lake, the roads were channels of liquid mud. . . . The confederates had evacuated their works during the night. We soon entered them and watched the blue lines of the federal infantry as they marched with banners flying into the town of Williamsburg to the sound of exploding magazines and caissons. Shortly after the General's [McClellan's] staff came in by a broad, fine street, bordered with acacias. All the shops were shut, but the inhabitants were for the most part to be seen in their doorways and windows, looking on us with a sombre, anxious air. . . . From all the public buildings, churches, college and the like waved the yellow flag. They were crowded with the wounded

left by the enemy. . . . The wounded were lying upon the very steps of the college porticoes.

During the peninsula campaign, Robert Knox Sneden, a Union private, kept a journal and sketches of his participation in the war. Sneden, originally a member of the New York 40th Volunteers, was a draftsman, surveyor, and architect. Assigned to General Samuel P. Heintzelman's III Corps mapping department, Sneden spent his time drawing and painting maps and illustrations of the terrain the Army of the Potomac traversed. Sneden illustrated the peninsula campaign and wrote extensively about it during his participation in the fighting and marching.

The peninsula's unpaved roads turned to seas of red, sticky mud that splashed onto everyone during the march from Hampton to Yorktown to Williamsburg in late April and early May. Sneden's account of the campaign tells of alternating days of chilly, rainy weather and then hot, humid, sunny periods. Roads became seas of muck with wagons sinking axle-deep into the goo. Cavalry units, riding by infantry troops, covered them with splashed, red Virginia mud. When the Williamsburg Battle ended early on May 6, Confederate troops retreated toward Richmond with McClellan's troops following slowly, in part due to McClellan's own caution, in part due to the poor roads and poor modes of transportation. Even with information supplied by contraband from around the peninsula, Union forces did not have sufficient intelligence about the terrain from Williamsburg westward.

Williamsburg residents believed the worst of the Yankees, as they called them. To their surprise, however, McClellan ordered his men to refrain from any harassment of the townspeople, even stationing guards at houses' gates to keep miscreants from doing damage to the homes. Dr. Galt, still directing the hospital for the insane, asked that the building be included within the limits of protection that McClellan set out. House searches occurred, during which Union officers and men looked for Confederates in hiding and contraband, escaped slaves or material contraband such as ammunition or weapons. In early searches, Union men displayed respect and care for the houses and their occupants. Union troops set on only abandoned houses and buildings, leaving alone those places that were occupied.

The city's streets, always a problem for its residents—muck to the knees in rainy weather and dust to the ankles in dry—gave rise to many complaints over the centuries until the Civil War. But on Richmond Road (originally the Old Stage Road) a tavern developed by one of the major mudholes, actually a pond more than a mudhole. Recognizing an opportunity when it presented itself, the proprietors began using the annual crops of frogs to prepare tasty frogs' legs and other frog delicacies for their patrons, thus the tavern's nickname—the "Frog Pond Tavern." By the time of the Union's seizure of the city in May 1862, the proprietor was a man called Old By Jucks. As the advance Union troops moved toward his tavern, he raised a white flag, stood on the steps, and invited the men in for some refreshment. The story illustrates the pragmatism of the city's nineteenth-century residents.

Although the Civil War became ever more savage in its destructiveness, ever more angry and hate-filled as time passed, there were still times when opponents could renounce their hostility to each other. One example is the summer 1862 wedding of Margaret Durfey to Captain John Lea of the Confederate Army. Lea asked that his old West Point classmate and good friend Union Captain George Custer be his best man. Custer, with McClellan's army as it fought its way toward Richmond that summer, gladly took the time to be with his friend in Williamsburg when the wedding took place in August 1862. Lea, injured in the Williamsburg battle, recovered at Bassett Hall, one of the many makeshift hospitals in the town that tended injured officers and men from both sides. Other hospitals included Bruton Parish Church, the Main Building (now called the Wren Building) of William and Mary, and private homes like Bassett Hall.

Custer reported in letters to his sister he wrote from the city that he spent a very pleasant two weeks with his friend and new bride. They played cards, sang songs, and generally enjoyed themselves before returning to the horrors of war. He also reported that the bride, Margaret Durfey, daughter of the then-owner of Bassett Hall, Confederate Colonel Goodrich Durfey, forgot to respond to several of the questions during the marriage ceremony. She, however, said after it was over that she had done so deliberately so as not to be bound by any obligations. Events such as this one ameliorated the boredom and horror of the war itself.

Two weeks after the wedding Custer returned to McClellan's forces, by that time back at Williamsburg and Fort Monroe from the failed "On to Richmond" campaign, while Lea, exchanged for a Federal prisoner, eventually rejoined the Confederate army and fought to the end of the war in April 1865. The two men represent an example of how the war divided brother from brother, father from son, wife from husband, mother from daughter, and friend from friend.

In the meantime, in Williamsburg itself the newly-reconstructed Wren building partially burned on September 8, 1862. The next morning a Confederate raid so angered Union troops that they finished the job, burning the building to the ground in retaliation for the raid led by Colonel William Shingler. The building, just rebuilt in an Italianate style after its 1859 destruction by fire, had been a military hospital and lookout post for both Confederate and Union forces.

Williamsburg

Union occupiers during the war tore down untenanted frame buildings to use for firewood; similar fates were met by unoccupied brick buildings as their bricks were used to build fireplaces and chimneys for enlisted men's huts and officers' quarters. The Governor's Palace's two office buildings, which had survived the fires and destruction of the Palace itself, met such a fate as their bricks were taken for construction purposes. Once McClellan pulled his army out of the city, it remained in the hands of the 5th Pennsylvania Regiment. As during the summer, that fall there were a number of fires that broke out in and around the town, destroying many frame buildings. Some Union soldiers wanted to burn the whole town, but their officers prevented them.

Union commanding officers settled into a three-story brick house called the Vest Mansion, located on the south side of Duke of Gloucester Street and next to what had been the Capitol building. The house, named for William W. Vest, treasurer of the asylum, had ample space as headquarters for both Confederate and Union commanders. Both Magruder and Joe Johnston, Confederate commanders, had used the house in 1861–1862 as their respective headquarters and McClellan used it when Union forces took the city in May 1862. It remained Union headquarters in the city until the end of the war.

Vest bought the house from Carter Burwell in 1836 and fled it for Richmond in 1862 when Union forces seized Williamsburg. Ed Belvin, a Williamsburg historian, cites Union officer David Cronin's description of the house: "The Vest Mansion, known to Unionists as Vest House was first occupied by Magruder. It has three stories including the attic. Its size made it attractive. Probably no other building was retained during war so long."

During the rest of the war, there were repeated Confederate raids on the town, including the Vest House, and Union intelligence reports indicated that some townspeople spied for the Confederates and supplied them with information about Union forces. General Richard Busteed, Union commander in the town in early 1863, wanted to burn it. Forbidden by his superiors from so doing, he did order all citizens to take an oath of allegiance to the United States or face expulsion from the city.

An assault by Confederate General Henry A. Wise in April 1863 drove Federal forces all the way out of the town into Fort Magruder east of the city. Federal artillery immediately began shelling the town, awakening many inhabitants who were still asleep. Shells struck several houses on the eastern side of the town. Townspeople fled to the city's western edge, hoping to escape the shelling. Wise and his men withdrew to the western reaches to escape the shelling also, then withdrew in mid-April towards Richmond. Conditions became quieter through the rest of 1863.

In early 1864 Union commanders again decided to attack Richmond from the peninsula. As earlier in the war, the commanders ordered town citizens to take an oath of allegiance to the United States or leave the city. Many packed up to do just that when word came that no such oath was necessary. A similar situation applied in fall 1864 and this time those loyal to the Confederacy had to leave, only to find out later that no oath was needed. Union commanders consistently vacillated among demanding loyalty oaths or threatening complete destruction of the city or simply letting the citizens alone.

The end of the war in April 1865 left the city not only at peace but more impoverished than in the decades before it. Although the war preserved the Union and ended slavery legally and constitutionally in the United States, it left substantial problems for its citizens to address. Among the questions opened by war's end were how to reconstruct the nation (restoring Confederate states constitutionally), what would be the lives and roles of the almost four million newly freed slaves (men, women, and children), and how to rebuild vast areas of the nation, mostly in the South, destroyed by the war.

Williamsburg quickly retreated into the background again. She was unable, however, to resume her prewar life. Half her population was newly freed, due to the war. The other half had lost most of its wealth. Destruction of almost all wood buildings in the city compromised her romantic grandeur. The college did not reopen until 1869 when the Main Building was, once again, rebuilt. The insane asylum barely scratched along. The great fire in Richmond set by Confederate forces as they withdrew destroyed all public records for James City County and the large portions of the city located in the county. The Confederate government had asked when it moved to Richmond in 1861 that all public records for Virginia's localities be transferred to the capital for safekeeping. James City County records and those of the part of the town included in the county went as requested to Richmond and became cinders and ash in April 1865.

Destroyed in the fire were all deeds and other official land records. The town and county spent several years after 1865 trying through a variety of legal means, including processioning, to reconstruct pre-war boundaries of individual and public lands. City and county governments had to be recreated and public services restarted once the war ended. Lawsuits begun over these attempts at reconstructing land ownership often lasted until the end of the century.

Descriptions of the town tell of a sleepy, impoverished community over which a lassitude had spread. As George P. Coleman, one of the city's late nineteenth-century mayors, put it:

Williamsburg

Williamsburg, on a Summer [Day]

The straggling Street, Ankle deep in Dust, grateful only to the Chickens, ruffling their Feathers in perfect Safety from any traffic Danger. The Cows taking Refuge from the Heat of the Sun, under the Elms along the Sidewalk. Our City Fathers, assembled in friendly Leisure, following the Shade of the old Court House around the Clock, sipping cool Drinks, and Discussing the Glories of our Past. Almost always our Past! There were Men and Women who strained every Nerve, every Means in their Power, to help Williamsburg of the present Day, to supply the Necessities of Life to poorer Neighbors, to build up the College and procure Means of Education for their Children, but even they shrank from looking toward the Future. The Past alone held for them the Brightness which tempted their thoughts to linger happily. . . .

This quote, so often used by Williamsburg historians of the late nineteenth or early twentieth centuries captures only part of the truth about the city.

Although the city experienced the same fate as many other towns and communities across the conquered Confederacy, there were those who did look to the future, particularly the freedmen and freedwomen. The abolition of slavery ended Williamsburg's whites' dependency on slaves to perform the town's hard labor. But African Americans looked to the future in order to participate in the development of public education, public health, and other elements of life which they wished to pursue. During the era known as Reconstruction (1865–1877), more than 60 percent of registered voters in Williamsburg and James City County were African American. Blacks helped to reshape Virginia's constitutional and legal landscape during Reconstruction by working in Virginia's legislature for what they wanted: free public schools, enfranchisement of black males (at least), and a system of public health. Better agricultural practices and knowledge were also on blacks' agendas for improvements in the state and Williamsburg region.

Just as during slavery, blacks in the city performed many daily tasks necessary to the city's economy. African-American workers included watermen, oystermen, skilled carpenters, blacksmiths, coopers, butchers, barbers, gardeners, and unskilled laborers. Blacks tested their freedom at war's end by seeking out family members (often traveling great distances to find them); going on their own to towns, villages, and neighbors; getting married; and many other activities prohibited to them while enslaved.

Blacks founded their own churches, no longer having to attend their former masters' congregations unless they so wanted. The State Sabbath School Union was one of the first combination religious-educational associations organized by African Americans in Virginia, having a chapter in Williamsburg using First Baptist Church for its undertakings.

Blacks also pushed hard to get free schools started and, during the first generation of freedom, adult African Americans attended school in Williamsburg as rigorously as did their children. Due to lack of funds for public school buildings, however, the local school board normally had to rent private space such as basements or rooms in private homes for classes. Whites and blacks alike attended such makeshift educational facilities for the first fifteen years or so after the war's end. Not until economic recovery had arrived in the city did the town have sufficient resources to begin building a few schools. To aid in developing educational facilities northern folk began sending contributions to support schools until such time as Williamsburg could support them herself. During the 1870s and 1880s, education continued to develop in the city, but the Supreme Court's decision *Plessy v. Ferguson* (1896) declared facilities called "separate but equal" constitutional. The court legalized segregation not only in public schools with that decision, but in all public facilities such as restaurants, public transportation, and theaters. Williamsburg African Americans would have to do the best they could to secure monies and teachers for their schools.

In the meantime, between 1850 and 1900 Williamsburg's religious community experienced increasing complexity as more and more Protestant religions began churches in the town and, around 1900, Roman Catholics began settling in the town. They usually went to Newport News for mass early in the twentieth century, but by 1910 Newport News priests were coming to Williamsburg to minister to the faithful. Revivalism swept the city several times during that half-century. The city had by the end of the Civil War Baptist, Presbyterian, Methodist, African Baptist, and Episcopalian churches. Jewish families began settling in Williamsburg in the 1850s, the Hofheimers being among the earliest. By the early twentieth century, there were Roman Catholics, Jews, and many varieties of Protestants in the city, a town that had been almost exclusively Protestant before the war. After the war the African Baptist Church founded several new congregations on the peninsula, testimony to the increasing power that religion had for freedmen and freedwomen. By 1900, Mount Ararat Baptist (organized 1882), First Baptist, and Union Churches formed the core of African-American life in Williamsburg.

Williamsburg

Danish- and Norwegian-descended immigrants began arriving in the area in the late nineteenth century, adding Lutheranism to the religious mix in the region. Settling in the Toano and Norge communities to the west of Williamsburg, these communities became an integral part of the Williamsburg region by 1920.

William and Mary College barely survived the war. Not until 1869 was the Main or Wren building reconstructed after the fire that destroyed it in 1863. Enrollments and income were way down, even after the completion of the Main building. The college limped along under the direction of President Ewell, who resumed his office after his service in the Confederate army. Despite his valiant efforts, the college did not recover during the 1870s or 1880s. To support the school, Ewell sought to raise private or public funds as well as recruit students. During these hard times there were many proposals to move the college or merge it with other schools well outside eastern Virginia, but local residents fought hard to preserve the college in its location.

Fortunately, someone remembered that in the early eighteenth century one Mary Whaley had left a small endowment for educational support in Bruton Parish in memory of her son Mattey. That sum, totaling about $8,000 by the 1870s, was used to support some grammar school boys from the town and to build a new building on the campus. In a directory of the town published just before 1900, several businesses are listed with capital seldom in excess of $8,000, so that sum of money must have done much for William and Mary during its time of need.

Although the northern economy suffered very little during the war (indeed some historians argue it expanded), the southern economy collapsed. Its currency became worthless, even before war's end. Its industrial and railroad systems were destroyed and, although casualties were less than those in the north, the percentage of casualties of able-bodied men was far higher. It took over one generation after war's end before its economy revived.

Williamsburg was no different. The peninsula sustained a very high level of destruction during the war, with enemy units fighting each other either in major battles or skirmishes nearly constantly during the years 1862–1864. The city itself was testimony to the destruction with most of its frame houses destroyed, many brick houses damaged or destroyed, and many public buildings also damaged severely. The college, as outlined above, provided little income for the city. The asylum had likewise fallen on very hard times. Government and market economies were also quite slim at the time.

By the late nineteenth century, however, things had begun to change in the city. New businesses began to blossom, especially those begun by blacks after the war.

Millers, blacksmiths, general merchants, and sawmills dotted the town as it began to revive from the doldrums of the post-war era. Although the population remained about the same, around 1,500, that population became busy serving a larger and larger clientele after 1880. New peoples moved into the region and after 1900 new busnesses introduced new lines of work and consumer products to the city. Between 1880 and 1925, the city experienced a modest boom that lay the foundation for the restoration.

Chapter Seven

WILLIAMSBURG IN THE RECONSTRUCTED NATION: 1880–1925

Between 1880 and 1925 the city underwent dramatic change in much the same way the nation itself changed. The nation completed its geographic integration when the transcontinental railroad system was finished by the early twentieth century. It completed the industrial revolution about 1900. Population grew dramatically and urbanization accelerated. The nation divided racially into a series of de jure and de facto segregated communities. In all of this and much more, Williamsburg shared.

The most important changes occurred in technology. A coupling of science and technology after 1860 in the Western world brought by 1900 electricity, telephones, airplanes, and automobiles. All this made its way to Williamsburg, along with new agricultural technology that dramatically reduced the work load for farmers and increased their output. Between 1880 and 1925, the city experienced a period of growth and development not seen in the nineteenth century.

Yet Williamsburg retained its reputation as a sleepy community resisting time and its blandishments. Two incidents, close in time to each other, helped perpetuate the image of a sleepy, droopy town. In June 1912, Williamsburg's officials forgot they had an election scheduled until an alert voter reminded them on election day of their duty to have the ballots prepared and ready for voters. But all this occurred on the morning of the election, so, as the printer began frantically printing the ballots, by about noon election officials reminded the city's leaders that state law required that ballots be prepared at least two days before an election. Printing them on election day would make the election illegal. The Richmond *Times-Dispatch's* editor had great fun with this incident:

> So, dear World at large, tread lightly on your path by Williamsburg, lest the drums and tramplings of your conquests weave, in the golden texture of her dreams, some darkling strand from off the sleeve of care. Why worry about election days when your head hangs heavy and your eyelids droop? Williamsburg wakes once a year to be sure that "The College" has a proper commencement. By some mistake of the calendar this year commencement and the election came in the same week. To do both justice was too much for Williamsburg, so Williamsburg went to commencement and then went to sleep. . . .

About a year later, another piece from the same paper described editorial reaction to a vote by the City Council that eliminated from the city's budget the $50 that the town annually paid the town clockkeeper to maintain and wind the town's clock in Bruton Parish tower. The editor, remembering the election day just eleven months ago, wrote:

> Once we wrote of Lotus-lidded Williamsburg, where the drowsy folk forgot election day. . . . Now the Lotus-burgers have come upon a way of solving all their troubles and of banishing carking care forever. They have seized on eternity and bound it captive; they have won immortality for all their dreaming. In short, they have decided to let the clocks stop. The City Council refuses longer to waste money having the clock in Bruton Parish tower wound.
>
> Time has always worried Williamsburg. The people didn't know what to do with it. There was so much of it; it was so persistent. They tried abolishing the calender, but time kept up. Now they will kill time by stopping the clock.
>
> There is a malicious rumor that the unwound clock has stirred many to a fever heat. This is a plain lie. The native Williamsburger never stirs. He never lets his anger be aroused for fear it should rouse the rest of him. He regards a fever as a breach of decorum.
>
> No one really believes that this town of twilight and dreams cares for the clock. It has too much sense. It doesn't care when it gets up—if ever, or when it goes to bed—if never. Everything can now be put off till tomorrow and tomorrow will never come. Belles, for whom the relentless passing of time made life miserable, can forget their birthday. Notes can be extended till Judgment Day. Commencement week at the College can be prolonged for months. Life will not be one thing after another. It will be just one thing.

These two incidents have become central to the myth of Williamsburg as the land time forgot. Lotus-landers, as citizens were sometimes called then, had actually begun a renaissance starting about 1880. The city's economy began to revive from the effects of the war and the depression of 1873 that had swept the country. The city's economy still rested on its traditional quadrangle of college, mental hospital, market town, and county seat, but much changed *c.* 1880 to stimulate the economy greatly.

Most importantly was the construction of the Chesapeake and Ohio Railroad. Collis P. Huntington built this railroad in order to get coal from western Virginian, eastern Kentucky, and other parts of the Appalachians. It ended at a set of coal piers in Newport News, but the tracks carried passengers and freight all over the peninsula. The company built a temporary spur line down the center of Duke of Gloucester

Williamsburg

Street in 1881 that carried passengers to Yorktown that fall for the centennial of the Battle of Yorktown that ended the fighting of the Revolutionary War. As soon as the commemoration ended, the company tore up the temporaries and laid permanent tracks just outside Williamsburg's northern edge.

In the 1890s, Huntington decided to build a shipyard near the coal piers at the eastern end of the peninsula; that shipyard became Newport News Shipbuilding and Drydock Co. and during the many wars the United States has participated in since then has done much of the shipbuilding for the U.S. Navy. The yard was originally to build colliers to carry the coal brought on the Chesapeake & Ohio to national and international markets.

At the time the railroad arrived in Williamsburg, almost two dozen merchants, two blacksmiths, and two mills (one corn and one wheat) supplied the some 1,500 inhabitants with food, merchandise, and services for horses and necessary iron utensils. Like so many other parts of the nation the railroad stimulated the peninsula's economy, bringing in new residents and encouraging the growth of new businesses and enterprises. By the early 1900s the town had grown appreciably, as had much of the peninsula. The town's population stood at almost 1,500 in 1880, grew to somewhat over 1,800 in 1890 and reached almost 2,050 in 1900. Part of the growth derived from immigration from Europe, especially southeastern Europe.

Internal migration, from one part of the nation to another, also spurred much of the growth. In James City County Scandinavians and Scandinavian-descended migrants began arriving from the Midwest and Great Plains in the 1890s. They had originally gone there after arriving in the United States from their homelands in Sweden and Norway. Railroad agents and land agents had recruited them with promises of good farm land and a warmer climate. They settled west of the town in communities now called Norge and Toano.

While agriculture remained the economic backbone of the area, the advent of the railroad and new businesses not only stimulated new enterprises but also modernization of farming and new farming undertakings such as vegetables and fruits for local and regional markets. Domestic animals continued to roam town streets until the early 1900s when city ordinances finally halted the practice of allowing cattle, sheep, and other animals to wander at will.

As the population began growing after 1880, rising from almost 2,050 in 1900 to over 2,700 by 1910 (an increase of about 80 percent in the thirty years since 1880), needs for services began to grow. This substantial population growth indicated the attractiveness of "Lotus-berg." The revival of the college contributed to the city's attractiveness. Limping along on next to nothing by way of income between 1869 (when it reopened after the war) and 1881 (when it closed because it finally ran out of funds), the college shifted from private to state-supported by 1888. Between 1869 and 1881, President Benjamin Ewell sought financial resources from whomever he might get them, with little success. In 1881 he closed the school, although each year he came to town from his farm in west central James City County to ring the college's bell to announce the opening of that year's session. He tried to keep at least one student (usually living in his home) pursuing some studies in order to maintain the fiction that the college remained open during those difficult years. Finally, elderly and tired, President Ewell retired after obtaining funds from the state to reopen the college in 1888 and Lyon G. Tyler, son of former U.S. President John Tyler, assumed leadership of William and Mary in 1888.

Tyler brought youth and energy to the college, including new faculty members and the beginnings of a state budget that provided for construction of new buildings, refurbishing of existing ones, and recruitment of new students. The new relation with the state meant that William and Mary began training teachers on a state budget and that the governor began appointing Visitors to the college's board, severing some connections that had bound town and gown during the eighteenth and nineteenth centuries. It also meant that women began attending the college's summer school teacher training program, an innovation that eventually would transform the college into a coeducational institution.

In 1906 the college became fully state-supported, with an annual enrollment of about 200. Students now matriculated from across the state, rather than the immediate vicinity as had been customary in the past. Tyler recruited new faculty, collectively called the "Seven Wise Men," all of whom came from Virginia. He also introduced in the 1890s a scholarly journal, *The William and Mary College Quarterly*, now known as *The William and Mary Quarterly*. Now in its third series, the journal is devoted to the study of early American history. With the women's rights movement acquiring strength and pressure for admission of women to higher education, William and Mary became coeducational in 1919. At that time and for several decades thereafter, William and Mary was the only coeducational institution of higher education in Virginia, attracting numbers of young women from all over the state as students.

During Tyler's tenure as president, eight new buildings, plus remodeling of the existing ones, added substantially to the campus. The rapidly-changing nature of the community required that the Board of Visitors ask Tyler that he stop allowing his horse and cow to graze at will on the campus. Not only the town but the gown was losing its rural, pastoral flavor in the early twentieth century.

Williamsburg

In 1919 Tyler retired and Julian A.C. Chandler assumed the duties of president. Chandler increased the student body from a little over 300 to almost 1,700 by the time he left office in 1934. The faculty grew from a dozen to almost eighty in the same period. At the same time, the student body became far more diverse as about 35-40 percent of it came from out of state by the time Chandler stepped down. Almost 50 percent were women by then, as well. Chandler also expanded the curriculum and spread of the college. The school went "off-campus" to begin offering courses in Richmond and the Tidewater, founding a branch college in Norfolk in 1931 that eventually became Old Dominion University. William and Mary began offering more technical and vocational courses to expand its curriculum while keeping its liberal arts and sciences focus.

While all this change was going on between 1890 and 1925, there was little friction between town and gown, with one exception. Once the city had started its public school system, it wanted to take over the Matthew Whaley School that the college had started as a model school. Although the city wanted to run Matthew Whaley, the college balked. Not until 1919 was a compromise worked out in which the city did take over the school, but continued to use William and Mary teacher trainees in it.

As William and Mary revived in the 1890s and early twentieth century, so too did the *Virginia Gazette*. Published in the eighteenth century as Virginia's only colonial newspaper, it had then an important role in the cultural and political life of the colony. Published only occasionally in the nineteenth century, the paper became a small-town weekly. In the 1890s, a William and Mary graduate, W.C. Johnston, took over as editor and publisher. A strong booster of the town, Johnston's editorial policy consistently supported economic development. He trumpeted each new industry that arrived in the community: a planing mill, corn and cob crusher, an ice factory, new banks, steam laundry, a knitting mill, and each new subdivision of the town, whether actually built and settled or just platted.

The *Gazette* published as a booster incentive in 1898 a directory of the city and county. Containing a listing of all the businesses in the city, it also had some county businesses, lists of citizens organized by race and geographic location in the city and county, and material on costs and curriculum at William and Mary. Advertisements for a variety of establishments were also printed in it. An advertisement for Samuel Harris, "The Leading Merchant of Williamsburg," noted that he sold "everything cheaper than anyone else." What the ad did not mention is that Harris was an African American, the leading merchant in the town (derived not from the ad but other sources). Harris was a black man who had relocated to Williamsburg from Richmond in the early 1870s. His Cheap Store, as it was named, was a general store in which almost anything fashionable at the time could be had. As a consequence of his business acumen, he owned a variety of enterprises and paid the highest taxes of any shopkeeper in town.

At the same time new philanthropical organizations appeared in the community, among them the Association for the Preservation of Virginia Antiquities (APVA), dedicated to acquiring and holding historic properties in Williamsburg and surrounding historic regions such as Jamestown. Among the properties the APVA acquired early on were the powder magazine and capitol grounds in the city and the presumed site of the first settlement/fort at Jamestown. Founders of the APVA included Williamsburg residents Cynthia Beverley Tucker Coleman and Mary Jeffrey Galt, two women dedicated to remembering Virginia's history. Their families, long-time residents of the city, had long been active in community, civic, political, and medical affairs.

Another important philanthropic organization, the Kate Custis Circle of the King's Daughters, founded in 1888, maintained a list of the needy and impoverished, providing as resources allowed firewood, Christmas presents, money, and food to those most in need. The founding members included wives of William and Mary faculty (Mrs. Thomas Jefferson Stubbs, for example) and other prominent women of the community. The Circle sustained itself since its foundation with monthly dues, beginning with 3¢/month and raising them first to 5¢ and then to 10¢ between 1888 and 1919. The ladies of the Circle also tried to find medical help to treat diseases such as pellagra when they afflicted the poor.

Other townswomen embarked on larger geographical journeys, as they departed for the west in order to teach. Minnie Brathwaite and Susan Garrett (the sister of one of the "Seven Wise Men") went to Indian reservations to teach during the late nineteenth and early twentieth centuries. Garrett returned to Williamsburg, having married Peyton Randolph Nelson, a direct descendant of Thomas Nelson Jr., a signer of the Declaration of Independence. Once back in Williamsburg, they settled in Tazewell Hall, now the site of the Williamsburg Lodge. Nelson became a "town character," driving his cows onto the palace green to graze and sporting long beard and hair.

The town's young women in the early twentieth century, however, wanted education. In 1908, a private girls' high school opened, only to close eight years later in 1916. By that time public schools were more widespread and girls and young women were able to obtain more substantial educations.

One of the young women desiring education was Georgia O'Keeffe. Her family moved to Williamsburg in 1903 when she was six years old and her father became manager of the local creamery. They remained in the town until 1912 when they moved to Charlottesville. Her father originally bought Wheatlands, a large frame house, but later sold it after he had made a sufficient number of concrete blocks to build a two-story concrete block house on Scotland Street. Georgia, one of eight children, was a solitary child who enjoyed painting. She continued acquiring skill as a painter, especially after the move to Charlottesville. She met Alfred Stieglitz in 1917; he was thirty-three years older than she. After a brief affair, they married in 1924. She moved to New Mexico after his death where she remained until her own death in 1986. She returned to Williamsburg at least once—in 1937 to receive an award and have a one-woman show of her artwork at the newly-created Department of Fine Arts at William and Mary.

O'Keeffe violated almost every standard of feminine behavior of the time, according to an anecdote told by William O. Stevens. In the late nineteenth and early twentieth centuries there were no legs on women. The only things that had legs in those days were "furniture, boys, and other animals." He recounts that the Queen of Spain at that time received as a gift several pairs of stockings. They were sent back to the donor with the curt remark: "The Queen of Spain has no legs." Stevens concluded that Virginia ladies had no legs then, either. To illustrate his conclusion, he tells the story of the local belle who, on a hot summer evening in the 1890s, lifted the hem of her floor-length skirt a few inches to scratch a mosquito bite. Damned as a "fast woman" by "polite society" for the rest of her life, she remained single to the time of Stevens's writing in 1938. "Under the code a girl might be a feline compound of malice and a notorious purveyor of scandal; she might lie like a small-college catalogue; she might be a monster of selfishness, and she could still be a lady. But anyone who could lift the hem of her skirt two inches to scratch a maddening mosquito bite—Oh, the hussy!"

As women pressed for extensions of their rights and freedoms, so too did African Americans. For the freedmen and freedwomen of Williamsburg and the United States in the late nineteenth century, life had possibilities. Between 1865 and the early 1890s, blacks had opportunities for economic, political, and cultural expression that were suddenly cut off to them when legal segregation, called euphemistically "Jim Crowism," appeared during the 1890s and early 1900s. They could travel without restrictions, they could buy property or set up their own businesses, they could attend schools and get educations, and they could participate, both as voters and as officeholders, in politics.

But African Americans, having tested their freedom and independence for two decades, suddenly found themselves cut off from the political, educational, civil, and legal rights they had expected would be consequences of slavery's abolition during the Civil War. Although black merchants like Samuel Harris might have done the most business in the city by the 1890s, by World War I, Jim Crowism was fastened onto the city just as it was in so many other parts of the nation.

The wave of segregation legislation, begun in the 1890s, was completed in most states by about 1905. But the federal government during Woodrow Wilson's presidency (1913–1921) reinforced segregation as Wilson himself ordered that white officeseekers replace blacks in the government. By 1915, the federal government was almost lily white.

In Williamsburg, black shopkeepers continued in business after 1900, but their trade was increasingly confined to African Americans. Although there were still black-owned businesses on Duke of Gloucester Street when the restoration began in 1926, they served mostly black customers. Occupations for black men included porters, drivers, day laborers, painters, janitors, and other menial jobs. Some African Americans worked as cooks, railroad men on the C&O Railroad (laying track and doing track maintenance), and watermen.

To counteract the effects of "Jim Crowism," Williamsburg-area African Americans formed their own societies and organizations. A Colored Odd Fellows Hall, located on the corner of Nicholson and Botetourt Streets, provided a gathering place where everything from philanthropic plans for needy blacks to local news could be discussed. That neighborhood was predominantly black at the time and places like the Hall and black churches in the immediate area gave African Americans places to gather. Blacks could provide insurance and financial needs to each other through organizations such as the Willing Workers Club and a Colored King's Daughters circle.

Virginia's 1902 Constitution so restricted the vote for African-American males that Williamsburg's black voting registrants dropped from over 190 in 1900 to nearly 40 in 1904. That constitution plus later state legislation restricted constitutional, legal, and civil rights for African Americans in the state and town by 1905. Theaters, restaurants, public schools, and public transportation became segregated during the "Jim Crow" era. By 1925, with the rise of the second Ku Klux Klan ten years earlier, not only blacks but many peoples of different ethnic backgrounds, such as eastern, southeastern, and southern Europeans, were targets of Klan violence and discrimination. In the city, white supremacy achieved new heights with the advent of Jim Crowism and the second Klan.

As Williamsburg segregated into two communities during the late nineteenth and early twentieth centuries, other segments of the city modernized. Water and sewage, electricity, and telephone services entered the city in the early twentieth century. The asylum changed its name to Eastern State Hospital in 1894; it had acquired running water a decade earlier and by the end of 1884 it had electricity. Williamsburg itself acquired a power plant in 1911 that provided electricity to the city government and private residents alike. By the end of 1916, a system of water and sewer pipes provided those services to any wanting them in the city. Connection to water and sewer were not mandatory, however, until 1917, when the city enacted an ordinance requiring all householders to hook up to the city's water and sewer system, citing public health as the legal reason for such legislation. In 1901, the newly-created Chesapeake Telephone and Telegraph Company built a telephone system in the city. The system relied on poles down the middle of Duke of Gloucester Street, an unsightly blemish the newly-created Civic League decided, but it took until 1932 before the company removed the poles, only after much pressure from Colonial Williamsburg and much to the relief of the Civic League.

Like so many other Americans of the time, city residents relied on kerosene for light until Williamsburg became electrified. So dependent on kerosene for light, cooking, and heat were town residents that the *Virginia Gazette* in 1905 could attribute a serious shortage that year to a plot by Rockefeller's Standard Oil to raise prices by withholding supplies. Even with that shortage, whatever its cause, the city did not pursue electrification until 1917, the year the United States entered World War I. Other modern "conveniences," such as public restrooms, began making their appearance in the city just before World War I. Advertisements for such public facilities consistently referred to them as restrooms and places for socialization, never mentioning plumbing or the specific purposes for which the hotels or public houses built them.

The automobile, appearing in the 1900s as a new mode of overland transportation, appealed to Williamsburg citizens. C.J. Person bought the first car in town around 1903 and began selling them in 1908. By 1912, there were several "infernal combustion contraptions" in town and the town had its first accident when W.A. Bozarth wrecked his Ford. His daughter Grace and two O'Keeffe girls, one being Georgia, were in the car with him. No one was seriously injured, but automobiles brought needs for new regulations, paved streets, roads, and highways, and new skills in handling the increasing speeds of which they were capable. Speed limits of ten miles per hour were established in the city, but given the nature of the town's streets, it is doubtful most vehicles could have gone that fast until paving began.

Another innovation necessary to the automobile age was the gasoline station. Entrepreneurs built several in town, especially after World War I. One of the more famous ones, the Peninsula Garage, was known as the "Toot-And-Come-In," located on Duke of Gloucester Street. The station took its quaint nickname from a play on the Egyptian name Tutankhamen, whose tomb British archaeologists excavated in the 1920s. Until the city's streets were paved, cars easily got stuck in the muddy roads or in the snow drifts of the winters of the early twentieth century.

In August 1914 World War I broke out and President Woodrow Wilson asked that all Americans remain neutral in thought and action. He said he hoped to use his office to mediate the war and negotiate a peace, but with little success during its first three years. Wilson and his administration, however, remained anything but neutral during the years of U.S. neutrality. An Anglophile himself, Wilson repeatedly denounced German policy during the war and threatened U.S. retaliation for what he called German offenses. His administration also favored Britain and her policies, acquiescing in many British intrusions into U.S. affairs. The most volatile issue, however, between the United States and Germany was German use of submarines to try to counteract Britain's blockade of German ports.

In 1915, Germany agreed to restrict the use of her submarines. Not until early 1917, with both sides in Europe approaching exhaustion, did Germany reinstate submarine warfare in an effort to win the war. With Germany's renewal of unrestricted use of submarines, Wilson could not remain out of the conflict. Germany's use of attack submarines to sink enemy shipping often resulted in loss of American life, for the ships often carried American passengers. In April 1917 Wilson asked Congress for a declaration of war against Germany, the strongest of the Central Powers (Germany, Austria-Hungary, Ottoman Turkey, and Bulgaria).

When Congress voted for the war declaration, it also provided monies to accelerate American armaments production. The peninsula once again found itself at the center of a war, this time not as combatant, but as gathering point. The Du Pont Company bought some 4,000 acres of land on the York River just before war broke out in order to construct a dynamite plant there. The government federalized the plant when the United States entered the war and converted it to a munitions loading facility. A community of homes for Du Pont workers already existed close to the plant, but that now expanded, for the federalized plant employed some 10,000 people. The new community, called Penniman, provided housing for the employees. When the war ended in November 1918, however, the government demobilized as rapidly as it had mobilized the year before. Eventually the area became Cheatham Annex and the Naval Weapons Station.

As the peninsula went onto a war footing, Williamsburg real estate brokers, agents, and developers immediately began planning extensive subdivisions on the eastern outskirts of the city close to Penniman and the plant. The war ended too soon for most of those to be built, although as population grew in the 1920s (especially with the restoration), some of them revived. During the war, however, there was a good deal of fraternization between the local populace and the men coming from all over the country to ship out through Newport News to Europe. Servicemen occasionally even camped on the greens in town when they had some time off from their training. During the little more than a year in which the United States participated in World War I, the military buildup on the peninsula created Hilton Village in modern-day Newport News to house government-hired shipyard workers who built Navy ships for the war effort. The government plant at Penniman brought about 10,000 new workers to the Williamsburg area. The large number of troops leaving for France from the peninsula also did much to introduce Williamsburg to a more modern world.

Local men and women not called up to serve did their parts through preparing bandages, finding cloth for uniforms, learning first aid to minister to the wounded who returned from France, and giving up meat or wheat on given days of the week in order that the troops in France might have plenty to eat as they prepared for battle against the Germans. They planted victory gardens to increase supplies of fresh foods for their own tables so that more foods could be sent to the troops. All this came at a cost as everything German fell victim to British and U.S. anti-German propaganda. The teaching of German in schools was halted temporarily. But the war also brought opportunity to make substantial amounts of money in the town and, had it lasted longer, would have provided many long-term possibilities for enrichment. Some property owners who rented to war workers tried to gouge them, but they were often warned by government officials about the consequences of such activities. When the fighting ended on November 11, 1918 (called then Armistice Day, now Veterans' Day), the area quickly resumed its peacetime activities. But a military presence, begun with Fort Monroe early in the nineteenth century, now became a fact of life on the peninsula.

Religious life in Williamsburg proliferated as the twentieth century began. Whereas the city had had only a few Protestant religions at the turn of the nineteenth century, there were not only many new Christian churches, but many variations on older religious themes when the twentieth began. Lutheranism appeared in the late 1890s when Scandinavians, arriving from the Midwest and Great Plains, established their own congregations in the Norge-Toano area. By 1910, the earliest Lutheran church had already split into two congregations, although served by one pastor at the time.

African Americans formed their own congregations, especially as segregation broadened and deepened in the area after 1900. Black churches, largely Baptist in denomination, included First Baptist, Mount Ararat, and Union in the town itself. Black churches provided social and cultural centers in addition to serving religious needs for black families. African-American churches were settings for weddings, funerals, plays, meetings, suppers, revivals, and a variety of other social/cultural activities in the early twentieth century.

As noted in Chapter six, Roman Catholics began settling in Williamsburg late in the nineteenth century. A priest from Newport News began saying mass in late 1908 in Cameron Hall, the social center of Eastern State Hospital. Some patients as well as a few townspeople were Catholic and attended the masses. A growing number of William and Mary students were also Catholic and they began meeting in the chemistry laboratory for their own worship services in the 1920s. Not until 1932 was there a formal structure dedicated to Catholic services erected in the town.

Bruton Parish Church continued as the sole Episcopal church in the community, but in 1903 the Reverend W.A.R. Goodwin arrived as rector. Serving until 1909 in his first stint in Williamsburg, Goodwin quickly made a mark in the community by organizing and directing a renovation of Bruton Parish Church. The church, changed greatly physically during the nineteenth century, especially in the 1838 renovation, needed much maintenance. But Goodwin persuaded the congregation that a full-scale restoration of the building to its eighteenth-century style would make it more attractive. That restoration, completed for the 1907 tercentennary commemoration of the Jamestown settlement, removed the nineteenth-century additions, restored the interior much as it had been in the eighteenth, and produced a description and history of the building. In one sense, the restored church was a first step in recreating the physical being of eighteenth-century Williamsburg, what eventually came to be called the restoration.

In 1909, Goodwin left the rectorate of the Bruton Parish for a similar pastorate in New York. He still dreamed, however, of returning to Williamsburg and trying to restore the town to its colonial grandeur. He got his chance in 1923 when William and Mary President Chandler invited him to become head of the college's endowment campaign. A few years later, he was once again rector of the church, but now had made contact with John D. Rockefeller Jr., himself a Baptist. It was in his contacts with Rockefeller that Goodwin finally found the "angel" he needed to finance his dream of colonial restoration.

Chapter Eight

WILLIAMSBURG REVIVED: THE RESTORATION, DEPRESSION, AND COMING OF WAR

In the mid-1920s the City of Williamsburg became the subject of one of the most interesting historical experiments conducted in the United States when Reverend W.A.R. Goodwin convinced John D. Rockefeller Jr. to finance a full restoration of the town to its eighteenth-century style. The town, for over a century languishing in romantic decay, had only lately awakened to the possibilities inherent in its earlier history. From the late nineteenth century until the beginning of the restoration itself, there had been efforts at reviving the town based on its history, and commemorations of the settlement of Jamestown in 1807, 1857, and 1907 stimulated further interest in such projects.

As pointed out in the previous chapter, Reverend Goodwin was instrumental in beginning the restoration. He developed over the time he spent as rector of Bruton Parish Church in the first decade of the twentieth century and then as endowment director and professor of religion at William and Mary a vision of the town restored to its historic centrality. His vision was not anchored solely in historic preservation, however, for he wanted the restored town to become a shrine to the ideals and values upon which the Republic was built. He believed passionately in those democratic ideals, even though the city and the rest of the nation belied the most fundamental of the ideals through the practice of segregation and discrimination against African Americans.

Born and raised in Nelson County, Virginia, Goodwin was a farm boy. He went to Roanoke College, then Virginia Theological Seminary. Rector of a small Episcopal church in Petersburg, Virginia until 1902, he then served Bruton Parish Church until 1909. Very strong willed, Goodwin struggled to start preservation of the city's antiquities, especially Bruton Parish Church itself. By 1907 he succeeded in restoring that church to its colonial style and furnishings. He published a report of the activity, including the steps and resources used to restore the building.

In 1909 he left the city for Rochester, New York, to serve as rector in its Episcopal church. He remained fourteen years, returning to Williamsburg in 1923 to assume new duties as head of William and Mary's endowment fund and professor of religion. His plans for inaugurating a restoration of the town had matured during his stay in

Rochester and in the next few years after his return to the city he sought to implement those plans. He applied to the Ford family for support, but his appeal was a bit too direct. In his appeals, he alluded to the fact that the building of so many cars, new roads, and new gas stations was one of the central issues in the 1920s decay of Williamsburg. The Fords, needless to say, spurned his advances. He then appealed to the Marshall Foundation, a corporation that did help Bruton Parish Church acquire the empty George Wythe house just north of the church and convert it to a parish house. To conduct the restoration of the house, he introduced the architectural firms of Thomas Tallmadge of Chicago and William Perry of Boston to the city. Eventually, Perry's firm would do the architectural work of the restoration.

In February 1924, at the sesquicentennial anniversary of Phi Beta Kappa, founded at William and Mary in 1774, Dr. Julian Chandler, William and Mary's president, was to go to New York City to deliver a major address at the commemoration. At the last moment he could not go, so he sent Goodwin instead. The speech called for the construction of a memorial at William and Mary and John D. Rockefeller Jr., himself a member of the society, attended the dinner and speech. Afterwards, Goodwin asked Rockefeller for money to construct the memorial and invited him to Williamsburg to see the town and the area. In the same year, Goodwin established a holding corporation for the purpose of purchasing buildings for a colonial restoration of the town.

Rockefeller with his wife and three sons visited the Tidewater in spring 1926. They toured the area, stopping to see Hampton Institute (private college for African American youth), Jamestown, Yorktown, and Williamsburg. In fall 1926, Rockefeller returned to Williamsburg to attend the dedication of the Phi Beta Kappa Society's memorial and during the visit he asked to be left alone to wander through the town by himself. At dinner that night, he told Goodwin that he was ready to proceed, but was not committing to the project completely yet. The first step was to finish refurbishing Bruton Parish Church, but, in the meantime, he instructed Goodwin to begin quietly buying historic properties in the town. During the next two years, Goodwin quietly bought those properties Rockefeller directed him to, the first being the Ludwell-Paradise House on Duke of Gloucester Street. Not until November 1927 did Rockefeller agree fully to support the restoration. By that time Goodwin had acquired over sixty-five properties in Williamsburg.

Goodwin, committed to keeping secret Rockefeller's participation in the project, went about town after dark carefully measuring lots and buildings to report their sizes and assist in collecting architectural information for the newly-hired architectural firm of Perry, Shaw, and Hepburn of Boston. Perry was to prepare architectural drawings for restoration of the buildings to their colonial-era style. Not only would this often involve extensive interior redoing, but removal from exteriors of nineteenth-century additions. There is a story that one dark night Goodwin scared a drunk when the metallic measuring chain being used to measure a foundation rattled, startling the tipster on his way home.

As time passed, townspeople began wondering how a rector of an Episcopal church could possibly have the money to buy all the properties he was acquiring. Finally, after rumors and unrest spread through the town, Rockefeller authorized Goodwin to announce what was happening. In June 1928, Goodwin told a town meeting who was buying all the properties and for what purpose the properties were being purchased. The townspeople discussed the meaning of the event, wondering what would be the consequences for their community as it became a "company town." The townspeople approved the project in general, but many still had questions and concerns. Instead of producing commodities for sale as with Hershey, Pennsylvania (chocolates), or Pullman, Illinois (railroad passenger cars) for example, the town would be rebuilt as a shrine to the ideals on which the nation was founded in the revolutionary era.

Goodwin and Rockefeller wanted the restored town to be a monument to freedom. Additionally, the restored town would recreate the material culture of the eighteenth-century community. Buildings restored or reconstructed (as in the case of the Palace or Capitol) would demonstrate how colonials lived graciously. Furniture and other decorative materials would enhance the image of the old colonial town. But their main aim, to use history to inculcate patriotism, has often placed the restoration at cross purposes with itself. What happens when historical reality (slavery for instance) belies the fundamental democratic, individualistic, and liberty-seeking truths that Goodwin and Rockefeller wanted Williamsburg to convey? Horace Mann, founder of the tax-supported, modern public free school concept, argued for using history as a means of inculcating patriotism among children in his curriculum for public schools in Massachusetts, his home state. He recognized that, unlike Europe, there were no governmental or other instutions in the United States that could do so, hence the public schools ought to undertake such a task. Other educators made the same argument, yet, for historians, the search for historical truth takes precedence over such uses as patriotic fervor. From the beginning of the restoration, Colonial Williamsburg has been in the middle of what is called today the "culture wars." Goodwin and Rockefeller, as primary directors of the restoration, gave it its guiding ideas and rationale, and were aware of the potential for contradiction in the presentation of their ideal, Goodwin especially.

Williamsburg Revived

For the next several years after the 1928 public announcement, the restoration tore up the town. One resident, John Arthur Hundley, wrote a poem describing reaction to the news of the buyout of almost 100 percent of the original colonial town:

> My God! They've sold the town,
> The streets will all come up,
> The poles will all come down,
> They've sold the Church, the vestry, too,
> The Sexton and the steeple:
> They've sold the Court House and the Greens,
> They've even sold the people.
> And you will hear from miles around
> From people poor and of renown
> My God! They've sold the town.

Residents generally supported the restoration, although older citizens of the community resented the intrusion on their formerly quiet lives. Many citizens initially resented, also, the idea of a northerner financing their town, especially when it came time to move the Confederate memorial from the Palace Green.

For a town used to celebrating and remembering its history, however, it was not too difficult to transfer historical remembrance from the Confederate to the colonial past. In a few years after publicizing the restoration, townspeople looked more to their colonial greatness when Williamsburg was the capital of a vast sub-empire. It may have been a bit harder, however, to regain a sense of nationalism associated with the presentation of the restored city as a shrine to the national ideals and principles of freedom, individualism, and republicanism after long devotion to the principles of secession and states' rights.

But city residents adjusted to the changes in ideas and principles more readily than they did to the physical alterations the town underwent between 1928 and 1936. As the Williamsburg Holding Corporation, Goodwin's original name for the company acquiring the lands and buildings of the colonial town, bought up the lands, many people, especially African Americans whose homes or businesses were located in what came to be called the Restored Area, were relocated to other portions of the town. In addition, white families who had long controlled the town's affairs strengthened their control, further segregating the city and enhancing white supremacy during the restoration and its aftermath.

An organizational plan emerged with the Williamsburg Holding Corporation retaining the power to buy and hold the properties, but Colonial Williamsburg, Inc.

was created to function as the non-profit educational wing of the association. Goodwin remained actively involved in the project, even though members of Rockefeller's own businesses and the Perry architectural firm took up responsibilities for restoration and development of the large-scale project. By the early 1930s, the project had generated several more corporations, many new departments and divisions, and a number of advisory groups.

In the meantime, the city's government began a study of its urban needs, resulting in a plan published in 1930 that called for new sewer and water systems and, especially, better roads. Paving existing city streets was high on the list of necessities for the town. Other problems included correcting drainage of raw sewage into ravines running directly from the city to the James or York Rivers, providinng adequate safe drinking water, improving trash and garbage collection, and in beautifying an increasingly unsightly environment contingent upon the erection of power and telephone poles. The impetus for this review of the town's infrastructure arose in part from the restoration and its leaders' desires for a congenial, pleasant environment for the expected visitors. City planning, so prevalent at the city's creation in 1699, had lapsed until the restoration began. From that time to the present, there has been active city planning in Williamsburg, the city adopting plans in 1953, 1968, 1981, 1989, and 1998. In the meantime, the city annexed substantial amounts of surrounding land, increasing its size from one square mile in 1722 to over nine with its last annexation in 1984.

As the city wrestled with the means to improve its physical image, the restoration continued hiring new people and creating new departments and divisions. Historical research, the province of Reverend Goodwin and some part-time assistants, gave way to a full-time department that assumed responsibility for researching the history of the town as well as each specific building. Harold R. Shurtleff was hired as the first historian of the restoration while Susan Higginson Nash, an interior decorator, was brought on to oversee selection of furnishings for completed, restored buildings. To work on gardens and landscaping generally, the restoration hired Arthur A. Shurcliff who had worked under Frederick Law Olmsted. These hirings and the many others that followed indicated the intent to provide as realistic a recreation of the colonial town as possible.

Researchers combed all available documents (although the City's and James City County's official pre-1865 documents had all burned in the fire that destroyed Richmond at the end of the Civil War). There was, and is, still plenty of historical and archaeological material for recreation of the town. Included in documents that restoration historians examined were insurance papers, deeds, wills, estate inventories, state tax records, letters, diaries, journals, surviving copies of the eighteenth-century *Virginia Gazette*, maps, etchings, paintings; any documents available to researchers were checked for material that might aid in restoring a house, public building, outbuilding, or garden. Since most other colonial towns, New York City, Philadelphia, or Boston, for example, had had most if not all their colonial buildings destroyed, Williamsburg became not just a shrine to the ideals of the Revolutionary generation, but the one town in which a glimpse of late colonial life might be had.

Like all other colonial towns, eighteenth-century Williamsburg had been a "walking town," one that could be walked easily in a day. Most residents in the eighteenth century knew each other by name and face. The same could be said for the town at the start of the restoration, but that soon changed as new people moved in to take up jobs in restoring the city. The population was just shy of 2,500 in 1920, showing a slight decrease from its 1910 level. By 1930, the population had reached almost 3,800 and by 1940 it stood at close to 4,000. The restoration accounts for much of the population growth and job stability during the Depression.

Although the town enjoyed more economic growth during the Depression (1929–1941) than at any time since the capital's move to Richmond, there was still a great deal of apprehension as the physical stage of the restoration reached its climax in the mid-1930s. In 1930 a rumor spread through town that Rockefeller might turn over the project to the National Park Service when the Palace, Capitol, and Raleigh Tavern restorations were finished. The rumor started during Congressional discussions in 1930 about building, under National Park Service auspices, a Colonial Monument road (called usually the Colonial Parkway) linking Yorktown, Williamsburg, and Jamestown, running along roughly the old 1620s–1630s palisade route that cut the peninsula in two to force local Native Americans off their homelands and to keep them from returning. The legislation, sponsored by Louis C. Crampton of the House of Representatives, designated portions of Jamestown, Williamsburg, and Yorktown as historic sites as well as setting off the road for construction of the parkway to link all three sites. Although the final version of the bill eventually stripped out the provisions associated with Williamsburg (except for the road right-of-way), the rest of the bill passed Congress in 1932.

Townspeople distrusted and disliked the federal government, in part due to the Civil War. They wanted nothing to do with the government, but, as events later proved, the discussions only considered creation of the parkway, the road linking the three points. The only lands acquired from the town were those necessary for the construction of the roadway. But some townspeople also disliked what Rockefeller was doing and refused to cooperate. Some balked at selling their lands; others deliberately altered their property to displease Rockefeller and those working on the restoration generally.

With the restoration going on constantly, the town was literally torn up. Duke of Gloucester Street was completely redone, taking out the central median, tearing up the two ribbons of concrete pavement, and removing all the power and telephone poles. The Mattey Whaley and Williamsburg High Schools, both standing on Palace grounds, were torn down to make way for the Palace's reconstruction. The Knitting Mill building, which had gone through several existences since the knitting business itself closed in 1910, was torn down to make way for re-creation of the Palace gardens. The Foundation had all utilities placed underground. A large tunnel was dug under the central part of the town for the Colonial Parkway, while the city obtained money to pave all the other streets of the restored area. The city government authorized closing the portion of South England Street that crossed the green just to the west of the magazine. The purpose was to restore the long natural vista from the Palace southward. The rumor, however, of the transfer to the Park Service proved to be just that. When Rockefeller bought Bassett Hall to convert to his own house, in which he lived two months of the year, one in spring, one in fall, the rumors of government takeover died. In 1933 many buildings opened to the public. These included the Capitol, the Palace, and many other buildings along Duke of Gloucester Street, often referred to as DOG Street. In October 1934 President Franklin Roosevelt visited the city, making a drive from the Capitol to the Wren Building (as the main building of William and Mary was being called), calling Duke of Gloucester Street "the most historic avenue in all America." With FDR's visit, Colonial Williamsburg in effect opened for visitors.

But all was not well. There were disasters associated with the restoration. Yetter recounts a story from architect Mott Shaw about the opening of Market Square Tavern:

> The opening day of the Market Square Tavern was a series of disasters! The beds hadn't come the afternoon the place was to open and finally they all arrived by truck and they had to be all set up. When that was finally fixed, some very prominent person appeared in an enormous Packard car (or a Cadillac) with a chauffeur. She was shown to her room and the plumbing didn't work. The chauffeur was placed in the little old stable and an electric fixture fell on him. Then, that night, the spare tires were stolen from the car which had been left outside in the yard. That is how those poor people spent the first night in the Market Square Tavern. It was a complete zero!

Williamsburg Revived

In the meantime, the Great Depression began with the crash of the New York Stock Exchange in September and October 1929. By the end of 1931, the United States and much of the rest of the world had plunged into the worst economic depression the modern world had known. Accompanying, even aggravating the Depression, was a series of severe heat waves and a long-term drought in the early 1930s. The most famous aspect of the drought was the Dust Bowl of the southern Great Plains, but in Virginia a heat wave, often with temperatures hovering around 110° in summer 1930 and 1931 brought agricultural disaster just as it had to the Plains.

Although the peninsula's economy still relied heavily on agriculture, economic change had brought the shipyard to Newport News and the restoration to Williamsburg; these softened the worst aspects of the Depression. The restoration provided employment for a large number of craftsmen, contractors, and service personnel during the 1930s. Reconstruction and restoration of buildings in what came to be called the "Historic Area" took up much of the rest of the 1930s. The town did not suffer as deeply from the Depression as did the surrounding rural region, however.

During the Depression, agricultural prices dropped so low that farmers in the Midwest burned their corn fields in the fall because it was too expensive to transport the grain to market. Dairy farmers poured their daily harvest of milk into local rivers and streams in Wisconsin, again because costs of transport vastly exceeded the prices they received for their cows' products. Similar stories are reported for the peninsula, thought not in such stark detail.

In 1933 William and Mary contracted with the Federal government to bring a Civilian Conservation Corps (CCC) company to the campus. The CCC was part of the New Deal. It provided opportunities for young men between eighteen and twenty-five who were unemployed and whose families were destitute to enroll in a company. Blacks and whites could join the CCC, but their units were segregated. Military officers commanded each company, usually enrolled at 200 men, and World War I veterans, no matter their age, could also join. The black company that camped on the college's grounds was charged with transforming some college woods into a park. In addition, the company worked to clean up from a 1932 hurricane that had done major damage to the area. The company also finished transformation of Lake Matoaka State Park and completed construction of an outdoor amphitheater at the lake. William and Mary and Colonial Williamsburg theatrical companies produced outdoor, summer-season plays on the amphitheater's stage. Another hurricane came through the area in 1938, destroying some local dams and flooding several roads as well as washing away others.

Williamsburg

The Depression did far less damage to the town's economy than it did in other parts of the peninsula because Rockefeller continued to pour money into the restoration. Some local residents remember the restoration as it got underway in the late 1920s and early 1930s. Ed Belvin recalls watching crews tear up the two ribbons of concrete and the median with the telephone/power poles between them that ran the length of Duke of Gloucester Street. He lived in the Peachy house at the northeast corner of Duke of Gloucester and Palace Green. Now called the James Geddy house (see Chapter three), the Belvins had to move in the early 1930s when the restoration acquired the Peachy house to begin its transformation into the Geddy house.

Belvin remarks that as he was growing up and watching the ongoing restoration, he became "aware of how important our little town was becoming." Although history was not one of his strong subjects in school (as it is not today for many students), he had the town's history drilled into him. Not until later in his life did he develop a fascination for local history and become one of the town's local historians. His father always had work during the restoration, but he and his siblings did a number of things to earn extra money. There was a ravine known as the "Bottom" running south from Main Street (Duke of Gloucester) to the James River. Belvin, his siblings, and other kids used to collect and sell wildflowers from it and hunt discarded pop bottles that they sold for refund. Among the entertainments the kids enjoyed were circuses and carnivals that went up on Courthouse Green during the summers and falls. But as the restoration proceeded, those entertainments soon disappeared.

One of Belvin's sharpest memories of growing up in the town was the shooting of the 1940 movie *The Howards of Virginia*. The film production crew used restored Williamsburg for many of the scenes and some of his friends got jobs as extras. Belvin confesses that all he did was follow Cary Grant wherever he went. Filming the movie in the restored area indicated how the town's importance increased as the restoration proceeded and word of it spread throughout the country. Belvin noted that an increased number of tourists came to the town, many from New Jersey or Michigan or New York complaining about how hot it got in the summers.

Belvin attended one of the two schools, Matthew Whaley, built on the Governor's Palace site before the restoration began. The other school, Williamsburg High School, was itself built right on the foundations of the old palace. He noted how many friends he made during his school years, never realizing that Matthew Whaley was an experimental school where student teachers from William and Mary prepared for their own teaching careers after their graduation.

As Belvin grew up, he watched the dramatic changes taking place on Duke of Gloucester Street as it transformed from an early twentieth-century business street to a restored colonial museum. He points out that because Judge Frank Armistead's house, Bruton Parish Church and churchyard, the palace green, and Courthouse and Courthouse green occupied so much of the north side of the street, businesses concentrated on the south side. Residences mingled with the businesses and, as had been customary in colonial days, several businessmen and their families still lived above their shops in second-floor apartments. To accommodate those businesses that had to be moved, the city and Colonial Williamsburg set off the block between College Corner and Henry Street. This region came to be known as Merchant's Square. Colonial Williamsburg researchers could find few sources to document what existed in that block in the colonial era, so the restoration felt comfortable relocating Duke of Gloucester Street stores and shops in the block to serve as a business center for the community and the tourists coming to visit the community.

As the town began to change in the early twentieth century, one group contributing to that change was the Greeks. Arriving from their homeland as part of an extensive migration of people from eastern, southeastern, and southern Europe after 1880, the Greeks who settled on the peninsula in the early twentieth century became restaurateurs. A substantial community of Greek families arrived on the peninsula during the first two decades of the twentieth century, many coming between 1905 and 1914 when World War I broke out and population movements stopped throughout Europe for the duration of the war.

Greek friends Tom Baltas and Angelo Costas were among the first to arrive in Williamsburg. They opened restaurants and other entertainment centers such as a bowling alley, a movie theater, and a pool room. Joining the small Greek community in the 1930 was Steve Sacalis, who also opened restaurants throughout the peninsula. Ed Belvin relates that Sacalis claimed kinship to Lafayette through marriage of one of his ancestors to one of the Marquis's cousins. Probably the most famous Greek restaurant on the peninsula was Nick's Seafood, located in Yorktown. Famous not only for its seafood, the restaurant also earned a reputation for its wall and floor mosaics. It proprietors Nick and Mary Mathews were proud supporters of the peninsula and contributed much philanthropically to causes in the area.

The oldest continuing business in Williamsburg is Bucktrout's Funeral Home, with business records reaching back into the mid-eighteenth century. Benjamin Bucktrout, the founder of the business, was a cabinet maker who also made coffins. From his coffin business, he branched into the mortuary field generally. The business remained in the Bucktrout family until the late 1920s when it was sold to Douglas Whitacre who in turn sold it to Clarence Page Jr. in the mid-1960s. It retained its name however. The town has many other businesses whose histories date back to the late eighteenth or nineteenth centuries. Most of them survived the Depression thanks to the restoration's consistent flow of revenue into public and private accounts. By the time World War II began, the city had begun to acquire a reputation beyond Virginia as a potential vacation and touring spot. Before commercial air flight took off, it was a convenient stopping place for vacationers heading south.

An unusual business in the Williamsburg area, and one that draws its own visitors from all over the country, began during the Depression when James E. and Gloria Maloney bought some land at Lightfoot, just west of Williamsburg. Maloney, a potter by trade, had studied his trade under Jamestown potter Paul M. Griesenhauer Sr. Maloney made the pottery and his wife painted it. They sold their wares along Richmond Road (later U.S. Route 60) and secured permission from other businesses in the area to market their products through them. After World War II, they added factory seconds, bought wholesale nationwide, and began marketing them as well. The business took off and became the Williamsburg Pottery, grossing millions of dollars of revenue yearly. These kinds of undertakings spread throughout the Williamsburg area after World War II, especially as visitors to Colonial Williamsburg grew in number from a few thousand a year (in the 1930s) to close to a million in the 1960s and early 1970s.

The opening of the first three restored buildings, the Capitol, the Governor's Palace, and Raleigh Tavern, during the early 1930s stimulated continued reconstruction and restoration. Early in the restoration, the emphasis was more on material culture as researchers in the fields of history, archaeology, decorative arts, and furnishings sought to make the restoration as authentic as possible. Few furnishings or other pieces original to the town's buildings, however, were found in Virginia, the nation, or around the world. Much of the furniture, glassware, dishes, and other interior furnishings were either acquired period pieces or reproductions themselves, leading Colonial Williamsburg, by the late 1930s, to begin marketing reproductions of furniture, glassware, dishes, and other types of eighteenth-century material culture. Carefully researched and often copied from surviving eighteenth-century pieces, this new addition to Colonial Williamsburg's revenue-producing repertoire was usually plowed back into the restoration, after expenses were deducted.

John D. Rockefeller Jr. oversaw all these developments himself. Visiting the town often in the 1930s, by late in the decade he and his family usually spent one spring and one fall month in the town. He kept up with new developments, even learning many details of restoration so that he would feel satisfied that authenticity was maintained.

Williamsburg Revived

As the 1930s continued, the town began to acquire a national identity, primarily by word of mouth. Leaders of the restoration hoped that early visitors would be so appreciative of what they saw and took away with them that they would tell their families, friends, and acquaintances about the village and encourage them to visit. By 1940, this seemed to be the case as several thousand people visited the town during the visiting season. By the time the United States entered World War II, the town had acquired a national reputation and during the war the restoration developed and implemented plans to bring large numbers of Army, Navy, and Marine officers and men to the town to tour it. They hoped, and the hope paid off, that the men and women would return after the war with their families to see the restored village.

In the meantime, during the Depression, William and Mary continued to function. It grew in student enrollment during the Depression, contrary to most other colleges and universities in the nation. During the 1930s, the college became approximately 50 percent female and 50 percent male and about 50 percent of students matriculated from outside Virginia. Students were overwhelmingly residential; few commuter students were admitted. Contributing to the restoration was refurbishing and restoration of the college's three colonial buildings: the Wren or Main Building, the Brafferton (originally built to house Native American boys sent by their families to receive a European education), and the President's House. The State of Virginia, short of revenue from the Depression's effects, could not provide its share of financial support. Yet the college continued to thrive, due in part to the fact that it acquired luster from its association with the restoration. The college's Library and Archives contributed substantially to historical research on the restoration. One of the most important documents of the restoration, the "Frenchman's Map," was found in the library in 1927.

Parke Rouse tells the story of how colonial historian Alan Simpson solved many of the map's mysteries. The map, drawn in early 1782, shows the city as it existed during occupation by Franco-American allied troops immediately after the Yorktown campaign. The map has been invaluable in providing Colonial Williamsburg historians, architects, and archaeologists clues and guides to where structures sat on city lots. Simpson concluded that the map had been prepared to provide French commanding officers information about places to board their troops. One of the anomalies of the map, the fact that it seemed to have two scales to it, Simpson explained by finding that the engineers who had made the map had paced it off rather than measuring it with chains. He concluded that one engineer paced north and south, the other east and west. He thought that each had a different length pace, hence the different scales up and down (north-south) versus right and left (east-west).

But one mystery about the map he could not solve—its maker. He considered a number of officers in Rochambeau's engineeering corps, but could find no evidence to link any one officer or group to the map. He did discover that a New York contractor, John D. Crimmins, gave the map to William and Mary College's librarian Emily Christian. All Crimmins could tell Christian about how he got the map was that he had been given it by a Union soldier who had taken it during the Civil War. What had been its history from its creation until the Civil War is difficult to tell.

In the meantime, the college had acquired a new president, John Stewart Bryan, in 1934. The timing was excellent as the college installed Bryan when President Roosevelt made his visit that fall. At the same time, the college conferred on FDR an honorary degree, further placing it in the national limelight. Bryan remained president of the college until 1942 when the Board of Visitors named historian John Edwin Pomfret the new president.

During the 1930s Bryan reemphasized the liberal arts and sciences nature of William and Mary, maintained the enrollment levels his predecessor had achieved, and toughened academic standards. He also encouraged the college to undertake more on-campus social and ceremonial functions, beginning Charter Day, for instance. His presidency introduced new departments, such as Fine Arts, that staged the Georgia O'Keeffe show in 1937. Bryan's contributions to William and Mary completed laying the foundation and much of the infrastructure, begun by Chandler, for the transformation of the college that would occur after World War II.

If white townspeople and the college population benefited from the restoration, African Americans did not. African Americans did not vote at the 1928 town meeting about the beginning of the restoration. African Americans who lived in what became the restored or Historic Area generally had to move out of their homes into other parts of town. As that happened, whites and blacks displaced by the restoration were relocated in racially segregated neighborhoods. Black churches in areas destined for restoration also had to move. The African-American Nassau Street First Baptist Church, a historically important nineteenth-century building, was razed in 1955 after negotiating relocation with Colonial Williamsburg. Although many more black than white families were displaced by the restoration, many blacks got jobs participating in the demolition or movement of buildings. Some stayed on in the restoration, taking on positions consistent with eighteenth-century slave work, such as cooks, liverymen, stablehands, cart- and draymen, and apprentice craftsmen.

One example of such activity is that of James Payne and his family. They portrayed themselves as slaves of George Wythe, living above the kitchen outbuilding of the Wythe property between 1939 and 1941. The family worked the kitchen garden and tended some of the onproperty livestock as part of their roles portraying a slave family in colonial times.

Williamsburg African Americans began protesting against Jim Crow segregation in the 1930s. At stake for African Americans like William H. Hayes, principal of the Training School, was better education for black children. The Training School itself was already overcrowded by the end of the decade. Badly in need of repair, it also needed new books and a more modern curriculum. Blacks also appealed to the NAACP to establish a local chapter in town, but that effort was not successful before World War II. They did, however, succeed in obtaining sufficient money and land to build Bruton Heights school, construction beginning in December 1938. Between then and the 1950s, Bruton Heights produced many African-American graduates who went on to college or into business, not just in the community but nationwide.

Bruton Heights School also provided a community center for blacks. They could not attend local movie houses, so beginning in fall 1940 movies showed once or twice a week in the school auditorium. It took another year, however, before the local school board approved expenditures for proper movie equipment (35 mm projector and large speakers) so that the movies shown, such as *The Howards of Virginia*, could be easily viewed and heard by large audiences. Weekly meetings of various black clubs and organizations met at the school and adult education became an important component of its service to the black community. When World War II began, many black teachers were immediately called up. But as the peninsula again became a center for gathering troops for the European theater, Bruton Heights became an educational center for black troops preparing to ship out for the war overseas. The school also became a black USO by 1943.

Blacks, economically better off than during slavery, continued to have to struggle against segregation to achieve personal and collective goals. Black schools remained substandard compared to white schools due to segregation. They still faced by World War II a segregated life, unable to eat in Williamsburg whites-only restaurants, attend movies in the whites-only Williamsburg theater, or go to a dance at one of the white dance halls in town. Their churches continued to remain centers of their lives, although by 1940 they also had Bruton Heights school as a center for activities.

The town's religious life changed considerably during the 1920s and 1930s. The first Roman Catholic edifice, St. Bede's Chapel, was constructed on Richmond Road near the college in 1932. William and Mary students had a large hand in getting the chapel constructed. In 1939, Reverend Thomas J. Walsh became the first resident priest of the chapel. African American churches experienced a boost when Elder Lightfoot Solomon Michaux bought land near Jamestown to begin a dairy farm. He also planned other enterprises for impoverished African Americans from the peninsular region, but they never reached fruition. However, Michaux was a radio churchman whose voice was heard in black homes across the nation.

One of the biggest changes in religion in the town came with World War II. With servicemen from all parts of the country and all religious denominations represented in the nation, the town had to find ways to accommodate those servicemen of faiths different from those in the town. But the town also saw an opportunity and the Rockefellers supported it. The restoration sought to introduce the servicemen and women to the nation's secular religion of patriotism and freedom through tours of the town. As churches sought ways to accommodate men and women of different faiths, the town introduced them to the principles of the nation's secular religion. By the end of the war, the foundation had been laid for a redefinition of the restoration's mission. The town would share in that redefinition.

Chapter Nine

WORLD WAR II AND AFTER: WILLIAMSBURG AND THE COLD WAR

From the late 1930s until December 7, 1941, residents of Williamsburg watched world affairs build toward war. In Europe, Fascist and Nazi movements led by their respective dictators Mussolini and Hitler plunged the continent into total war in 1939. In East Asia, Japanese militarists, led by Tojo, began war in China in 1937. The Roosevelt administration, responding to powerful public opinion, kept the United States formally neutral when fighting broke out; however, FDR himself wanted the nation to be prepared and more active on behalf of those nations attacked by aggressors. The nation was still in the grip of the Depression, but Roosevelt's desire to build up the U.S. military meant the beginning of rearmament, the means by which the nation finally recovered economically.

In Williamsburg, the restoration had proceeded through the late 1930s, continuing the reconstruction of the Restored Area, as the region of the town bought by Rockefeller for the Colonial Williamsburg Foundation came to be called. The message the restored part of the town was to deliver was two-fold—to show Americans the ideals of democracy and freedom the republic's founders had embodied and to demonstrate what life was like in the mid- to late eighteenth century. Most tourists, or visitors as Colonial Williamsburg began to call them, who came in the 1930s understood the nature of the messages, although many came to examine the material culture as well. They wanted to see the furniture, ceramics, cutlery, and other elements of daily life that had made up parts of the material culture of eighteenth-century families. Prior to World War II visitors enjoyed leisurely strolls through the restoration, only a few thousand visiting each year. The town was not congested and all the streets remained open to auto traffic.

But the city remained a segregated one, in which African-American visitors were welcome to the restoration, but had to stay in segregated housing and eat in segregated restaurants. African-American residents had been relocated during reconstruction into more segregated neighborhoods of the city, too.

U.S. participation in World War II launched changes, not only in the segregated nature of the city but in how visitors viewed and toured the restoration. During the war itself civilian tourism dropped to near zero, although peninsula residents could visit the facility and did. War-time rationing of everything from gasoline to tires meant that only local residents could take advantage of what the town had to offer. Moreover, substantial numbers of townspeople served in one or another of the military branches during the war, thus cutting the labor supply. But the peninsula, as it had been in World War I, became a major staging and training area for dispatch of troops to the European theater of the war.

City residents all "did their bit" for the war from acting as civil defense and air raid wardens to enforcing blackouts to providing used clothing to go to England for those families bombed out by Germany's air raids. Vernon M. Geddy Sr., a vice president of Colonial Williamsburg, coordinated the city's war efforts. During the four years of American participation in the war, townspeople did everything from making clothing, bandages, and other surgical supplies; building air raid shelters; entertaining wounded troops convalescing in area military hospitals; and raising money by purchasing war bonds. City residents willingly accepted rationing of important commodities like gasoline, sugar, butter, meat, and even coffee. Townspeople planted gardens to supply themselves with fresh vegetables in order that commercially-produced vegetables could be sent to the troops overseas. As in the rest of the nation those who did not go to war spent much of their time supporting the U.S. war effort.

In the area around the town, new military camps like Camp Peary, named for the arctic explorer Robert E. Peary, sprang up. The Navy acquired several thousand acres to build Peary. The camp prepared Seabees to construct quickly airstrips, military housing, and roads. The camp sent them to both major theaters of the war—European and Pacific. The camp remained a training facility for Seabees until 1944 when it added distribution of naval stores to its activities.

William and Mary became an ROTC facility. The college also established educational programs in a variety of technical and scientific disciplines to provide soldiers training for specialized missions overseas, instruction in intelligence gathering, mine and other explosives making and use, and other technical skills necessary in fighting the war. Students not in the military joined work-study programs that placed them for two or three days a week at a nearby military facility while they attended classes the other days. These kinds of programs at the college and in the city generally provided a sense of unity and common purpose not usually witnessed in the town or the nation.

As civilian tourism plummeted after U.S. entry into the war, Rockefeller and Goodwin turned to other means by which they might maintain public interest in the restoration. One way was to attract military personnel to the restoration, so Colonial Williamsburg officials began offering special packages to military personnel, providing them the opportunity to tour the town for free. As European dictatorships derided freedom and the principles of the Enlightenment, leaders of Colonial Williamsburg began to stress even more those very principles of reason, freedom, and equality embedded in the eighteenth-century Enlightenment and its offshoot, the American Revolution.

The tour program Colonial Williamsburg managers prepared for military personnel temporarily stationed on the peninsula was intensive. From Monday through Saturday, 9 a.m. to 4 p.m. each day, 300 armed forces members, mostly Army or Navy, toured the town. The idea was that all personnel at places like Fort Eustis, established on Mulberry Island in Warwick County, would have the opportunity to see the restoration and receive indoctrination about principles of freedom and liberty, principles for which they were fighting in the war itself. Financing for the tours came from Rockefeller himself who agreed to supply $300 per week to support the tours. The educational plan worked well, for many letters to officials of the restoration praised what the writer (soldier or sailor) had seen and learned from his or her experience.

Since the public could not visit the restoration during the war, the restoration decided to go to the public via radio. Rockefeller and other Colonial Williamsburg leaders decided to pursue a series of radio programs that would describe for Americans the importance of the princples of freedom, reason, and equality embedded in Revolutionary rhetoric. President Roosevelt recommended that CBS air the programs, but William Paley, CBS president, refused.

To foster further the military's ties to Colonial Williamsburg, Rockefeller recommended the construction of a USO building in the town. The hall opened in one of the newly-built structures on Merchants Square in 1942. A segregated USO club opened shortly thereafter in Bruton Heights School. Jack Benny and Bob Hope brought their shows to Camp Peary while Red Skelton entertained townsfolk doing street comedy on Duke of Gloucester Street.

One more development during the war involved the creation of the Institute of Early American History and Culture (now the Omohundro Institute of Early American History and Culture). Created under the joint auspices of Colonial Williamsburg and the College of William and Mary, the institute has become an important research agency for the investigation of early American history. The institute sponsors research by young historians interested in North American colonial history, publishes the *William and Mary Quarterly*, and provides a center for established historians of early American history to test out their ideas and new research.

Williamsburg

Many area residents fought in the war. A local American Legion post lists 884 men and women who served. At least twenty died either of wounds received during the fighting or on the battlefields themselves. The highest ranking serviceman was Rear Admiral John Lesslie Hall Jr., whose brother Channing was the city's mayor during the war. Admiral Hall was one of the Navy figures responsible for perfecting amphibious warfare.

Among those townsmen who lost their lives were W.A.R. Goodwin Jr., Reverend Goodwin's son. He died when his P-40 airplane crashed during fighting in Sicily. Dewey C. Renick Jr. died in March 1945, when his plane crashed somewhere in mountainous regions of the Philippine Islands. The *Virginia Gazette* reported servicemen's deaths. Word of mouth also transmitted bad or good news throughout the town. Retaining their small town atmosphere, most city residents knew and mourned the victim when the name became public.

The area also had its share of prisoners of war, kept at Camp Peary. In March 1945, three German POWs escaped from Peary and made their way into town. Cornered in some shrubbery, one of the three tried to run off but was soon recaptured. Their captors, A.E. Kendrew, restoration architect; Doctor A.G. Ryland; and Frank Dobson escorted them to the Williamsburg Inn where a local police lieutenant took them into custody for transport back to the camp.

The city also underwent substantial physical growth during the war. To improve transportation of people and materiél to the peninsula, the federal government widened U.S. Route 60 from Richmond to Newport News, passing through Williamsburg. Rail traffic increased, as did water passage. Airports came into existence on the peninsula as the need for military air traffic increased. The city's population temporarily increased as war workers and their families, receiving short-term assignments to places like Cheatham Annex (part of the Naval Weapons Station complex along the York River), Fort Eustis, or Camp Peary poured into the town and surrounding areas.

When news arrived on August 14, 1945, that Japan had formally surrendered, there was wild rejoicing in town. Restaurateurs and shopkeepers closed their establishments, though some restaurant owners did remain open and served their customers free meals for the rest of the day. People danced in the streets, telephone lines were jammed, and the celebrations continued well into night. The end of war, however, meant dramatic changes for the city and its environs, for over the next sixty years it became an international center for tourism, recreation, and the elaboration of the Americanism message that Rockefeller and Goodwin had set out to portray via the restoration.

World War II and After: Williamsburg and the Cold War

The end of war brought a sense in the nation that the future belonged to the United States. Harry S. Truman, who became president when Roosevelt died in April 1945, and his cabinet and other administration leaders behaved as though the United States would provide leadership to the rest of the world. The United States, an isolationist nation prior to World War II, was now willing to assert its power and dominance throughout the world. The country suffered no physical damage from World War II, contrary to the devastation in Europe, Japan, and East Asia generally. American military casualties numbered about 400,000 compared to the enormous military losses, in tens of millions, in Europe and Asia. The Nazi murder of Jewish and other "undesirable" peoples, amounting to about 10 million, added even more to the horrific loss of life associated with World War II.

American leadership, however, failed to understand the nature of the Soviet Union, an uneasy ally during the war. Russia had borne the brunt of the fighting in the European theater and twice in twenty-five years Germany had invaded Russian soil, taking millions of lives. Russian dictator Josef Stalin was determined not to let that happen again. In the five years following the war, he constructed a large buffer zone west of the Soviet Union, installing Communist governments in East European nations. He actively worked to keep Germany divided into two peoples and nations in order to maintain German weakness. The United States, interpreting Stalin's activities as a Communist threat to the rest of the world, reacted with the creation of a series of treaty systems called containment to keep Soviet Communism from expanding and taking over the world. The beginning of the Cold War brought a series of diplomatic, political, and military confrontations between the United States and the Soviet Union that ended only in 1989–1991 when the Soviet Union quietly collapsed and disappeared due to internal agricultural and industrial weaknesses, to be replaced by a Russian republic.

Colonial Williamsburg played an increasingly important role in the prolonged confrontation between communism and capitalism, expanding the domestic message about freedom and liberty that Rockefeller and Goodwin had originally created into an international one. By 1950, John D. Rockefeller Jr. was retired from the role of active manager that he had taken during the Depression and war. But he remained involved in Colonial Williamsburg's activities. His son, John D. Rockefeller III, had a wider vision of the restoration's role in cultural affairs. He believed that Colonial Williamsburg should become an international shrine to democracy, freedom, liberty, individualism, and self-government. His father and he clashed over his ideas. His father, however, ultimately accepted the new role for the Historic Area, while at the same time retaining his interest in overseeing further physical reconstruction of the town.

Williamsburg

By 1950, the nation had entered a period of intense anti-communism, culminating in McCarthyism. Colonial Williamsburg's emphasis on the positive ideals of the United States complemented the negative anti-communist mood of the nation. During the 1950s international leaders began visiting the colonial capital, including Queen Elizabeth II and her royal consort Prince Philip in 1957 as part of the commemoration of the 350th anniversary of the settlement of Jamestown.

Between the end of World War II and 1970, as Williamsburg became a center for international visitors, William and Mary became an internationally-known university. The town's population, which had stood at almost 3,800 in 1930, grew slowly to a little over 3,900 by 1940, to more than 6,700 in 1950, then reached more than 6,800 in 1960 and soared to nearly 9,100 by 1970. Part of that population growth was due to several annexations, principally from James City County. The annexations substantially increased the city's geogrpaphic size from its original one square mile. As the population grew, however, services and other needs did also. The city began to shed its small town quality as pressure for more services grew. Professionalization began to replace volunteerism in fire protection, for instance. The volunteer fire department slowly gave way in the 1950s to a paid, professional force. School needs expanded, especially as Baby Boomers began crowding into the city's elementary and high schools during the 1950s and 1960s. The city's residents debated and argued over growing taxes to pay for new additions to the city's school system. The city and James City County merged their school systems in 1953 to streamline administration and prevent duplication of costs, but population growth in both polities necessitated increased expenditures and called for more revenue. In 1961 Williamsburg Community Hospital opened; earlier hospitals had usually been privately-owned like that of Dr. Baxter I. Bell, one of Williamsburg's early twentieth-century physicians whose medical service touched almost everyone in town at some time in their lives.

By the early 1960s Virginia's higher education system had also entered the population crisis as more and more qualified applicants from within and without the state sought admission to Virginia's colleges and universities. To alleviate overcrowding William and Mary worked with the state to found new two-year branches, one of them being Christopher Newport College (CNC) in Newport News. That college opened its doors in 1961 to almost 200 students; it is now an independent, state-supported university with almost 5,000 students annually enrolled. From 1961 until 1970, CNC remained two-year; students successfully completing their sophomore year at CNC transferred to William and Mary to complete their higher education. This was another example of William and Mary's service to the peninsula and state.

World War II and After: Williamsburg and the Cold War

As more and more visitors came to Williamsburg in the 1950s and 1960s, the restoration's message of democracy, individualism, self-government, and liberty contrasted sharply with the reality of a segregated town. Although Reverend Goodwin had at the inception of the restoration called for an integrated presentation based on the fact that one half of the town's eighteenth-century residents had been slaves doing the vast majority of physical labor, that part of the town's history remained largely hidden until the post-war era.

Nationally, African Americans had begun fighting segregation in the 1910s and 1920s, but with little success. In the 1930s, the U.S. Supreme Court began hearing appeals of criminal trials in which one or another of the Bill of Rights played a part. In so doing, the Court began setting procedural guidelines for constitutional adherence to the Bill of Rights. The Court heard cases involving what the Constitution meant by a fair, speedy, and impartial trial. In many cases, the issues brought before the Supreme Court involved African Americans whose rights under the Bill of Rights or the Fourteenth Amendment had been violated. By the outbreak of World War II African Americans had a footing upon which to expand their fight to end segregation. The war itself added to that footing as blacks showed their commitment to the nation's principles for which they were fighting. When the administration ordered the armed forces desegregated immediately after the war, the foundation for the Civil Rights Movement was just about completed. The key event that finished that foundation was the public school desegregation case Brown v. the Board of Education of Topeka (1954), actually a compilation of five suits brought against a variety of public school districts including Prince Edward County, Virginia public schools.

The decision that ordered desegregation of all U.S. public schools "with all deliberate speed" took almost two decades after its rendering to enforce. Many white Virginia politicians and their supporters embarked on "massive resistance," a campaign to prevent segregation of local public schools. This involved closing public school systems in some localities where white resistance was most intense. The state dropped age requirements for quitting school and most Virginia school systems refused to integrate until forced to by court order. In the consolidated Williamsburg–James City County school system, integration came only in 1968. By that time the Supreme Court had also declared unconstitutional all other forms of segregation, including bans on marriage between blacks and whites.

The restoration had tried to adjust its national and international attraction to the customs of a southern, white-dominated town during the 1950s. It opened its doors more and more to blacks, especially as peoples from many different parts of the world began coming to visit. In addition to adjusting its policies on race, Colonial Williamsburg had to adapt to many other needs. In the late 1940s, the city agreed to close to vehicular traffic Duke of Gloucester Street and most of its cross streets from Merchants Square to the Capitol building. Colonial Williamsburg then had to acquire a fleet of buses to transport their visitors around the restoration. New attractions such as craft shops and general stores opened in the Restored Area to give visitors more options to participate in recreated colonial life (one could buy a reproduction of a pair of colonial handcrafted shoes or a cooper-made bucket or firkin or a Brown Bess musket). Restaurants and other accommodations were added to meet the growing numbers of tourists.

John D. Rockefeller Jr. had never intended that the restoration pay for itself in terms of visitor entrance fees, but costs of running the restoration spiraled in the 1960s and 1970s. He never believed the restoration should be for-profit. Fees had been kept low ($1.75 in the 1930s for instance). Revenues augmented Rockefeller's financial sponsorship and helped defray costs, but never approached break-even. In the 1950s and 1960s, corporate officials raised existing fees and added new ones in hopes of achieving break-even. In so doing, they threatened to curtail the number of visitors who came each year, many of whom thought the restoration was for-profit and was gouging them. The restoration became an almost year-round event, especially its Christmas celebration with the Grand Illumination. All the activity necessitated substantial outlays and investments, and income from the visiting side of the ledger seldom came close to matching expenditures. On the other side of the ledger, however, was income derived from restaurant, hotel, and gift sales, incomes that often exceeded expenditures necessary to maintain or improve those facilities.

Advertised as quality reproductions, furniture, china, glassware, flatware, and many other elements of eighteenth-century life were sold through the merchandising side of Colonial Williamsburg. Revenues from hotel and restaurant sales were always brisk, even as competition from independent and chain motels and restaurants made inroads on Colonial Williamsburg's accommodations.

Crowds began to grow in the late 1940s and 1950s, especially as service men and women began bringing their families back to the Restored Area to show them what they had seen during the war. They stimulated interest in colonial history; Anders Greenspan relates one letter writer who averred his son had learned more from his brief visit to Colonial Williamsburg about early American history than he had learned all year in school. The town increasingly became an integral part of the restoration. More and more blacks began working for Colonial Williamsburg as the restoration inaugurated programs to demonstrate slavery and the work that slaves did in the eighteenth-century town. The importance of that work was not lost on visitors, who began to see what contributions to the economic, cultural, and political beginnings of the country slaves made. Colonial Williamsburg programs also began providing imaginative reconstructions of interactions between slaves and their white masters and mistresses. These programs were a bit more risky than showing how slaves lived and worked in the community, for they not only were hard to establish in the documentary sources, but also might send the wrong message to their viewers, the visitors themselves.

As the city grew, so too did its religious life. During the 1950s, a Christian Science reading room was established. The first synagogue, Tempel Beth El, was founded in 1969. Bruton Parish Church, however, retained its place as civic and communal center, often serving in an ecumenical fashion for religious ceremonies that transcended religious borders in the community. Religious life was augmented with the creation of a Unitarian-Universalist fellowship that allowed each member to make his or her own religious exploration and journey. The richness of religious life in the city contributed to the intellectual and philosophical air that Rockefeller and Goodwin had wanted to establish.

Desegregation, growth of the college, expansion of the restoration's message and mission as well as its physical increase, new construction in town, professionalization of services such as fire and medical, and an internationalization of the city's appeal transformed the town in the twenty-five years after World War II. The last almost thirty-five years of Williamsburg's history has kept it a national and international shrine to freedom and liberty.

Chapter Ten

WILLIAMSBURG IN MODERN TIMES: 1970–2004

During the 1970s Williamsburg, like much of the rest of the country, suffered through the traumata of Vietnam, an oil crisis, and the Nixon resignation. New attractions appeared in the area, however—attractions that both competed with and complemented the restoration. The Cold War continued into the 1980s with continuous military buildups by both the United States and the Soviet Union. The peninsula remained an important element of the U.S. military with Langley Air Force Base in Hampton, Newport News Shipbuilding's continuing construction of naval vessels (aircraft carriers especially), Forts Monroe and Eustis, the Naval Weapons Station at Yorktown, and a CIA training ground at Camp Peary. The large number of military personnel stationed in the area gave a transient nature to the peninsula region, including Williamsburg. But military retirees also comprised a substantial core of those wishing to settle in Williamsburg, many of whom had been stationed in the area at some time during their service.

The completion of Interstate 64 and other primary highways encouraged the growth of vehicular traffic all over the peninsula. Between 1970 and the early twenty-first century, car ownership has more than doubled in the area, from about 0.3 cars per individual in 1970 to over 0.7 by 2000. By 2000, affluence reached the peninsula in ways those living on it in the 1960s or 1970s had never envisioned. The region has suburbanized without ever having urbanized (meaning there was no large or medium-sized central city such as Boston, or Sacramento). The region now has a large number of shopping malls, outlet malls, bedroom communities, and decentralized recreation facilities. As with many other parts of the country, it requires a car to accomplish one's "errands" on a Saturday.

Since 1970, the College of William and Mary maintained its growth and development, including granting its first doctoral degrees. It implemented and expanded four professional programs: marine science, education, law, and business. By the mid-1990s its student population reached over 5,000 undergraduates and almost 1,500 graduate and professional program students. The faculty grew comparably, although lack of funding by the State of Virginia during the whole of the 1990s and early 2000s has made its financial situation difficult, as is the case for colleges and universities throughout the state. To compensate, the college embarked on an ambitious fund-raising project to enhance its endowment. Four presidents have served the college since 1960: Davis Y. Paschall, 1960–1971; Thomas A. Graves Jr., 1971–1985; Paul R. Verkuil, 1985–1991; and Timothy J. Sullivan, 1991–2005.

The *Washington Post* reported on Saturday, June 19, 2004, that Sullivan announced his intention to leave the college's presidency in Spring 2005. The *Post* further reported that Sullivan will have served thirteen years as president, but his association with the college goes back to his undergraduate years; he graduated from the college in 1966, became a member of the Law School faculty in 1972, served as dean of that school from 1985 to 1992, and assumed the presidency in the latter year. Sullivan has succeeded in expanding the endowment fund, securing more research grants, and acquiring more private donations. The college enrolled almost 5,800 undergraduate and approximately 2,000 graduate and professional students for the academic year 2003–2004. Sullivan, the college's twenty-fifth president, has fought hard to maintain and enhance the college's position in Virginia, working to keep the state legislature from capping out-of-state enrollments that comprise over a third of total undergraduate student body and criticizing the state government for its parsimony respecting its institutions of higher education.

The college has acquired a national reputation that places it among widely-recognized higher education institutions of excellence. Its faculty and library are the backbone of its liberal arts and sciences undergraduate and graduate educations. From a small, liberal arts college attracting students largely from the immediate area in the eighteenth and nineteenth centuries, it has grown in size and reputation to a national and international institution through the work of its twentieth- and twenty-first-century presidents and faculty. Many of its faculty, such as James Axtell of the History Department, have international reputations in their fields of expertise. As the college grew, so too did the city.

The city's population increased by almost 1,000 between 1970 and 1980, reached almost 11,500 by 1990, and approached 12,000 in the 2000 Federal Census, giving it a population density of over 1,300 per square mile by the latter date. By adding to the city's population those areas collected into the unofficial "Williamsburg Area," there was an almost 100-percent growth in population between 1970 and 2000. This growth and concentration of population has meant, as Jack Edwards put it in *Change & Growth: Williamsburg Begins a Fourth Century*, "more homes, more grocery stores, more convenience stores, more fast-food restaurants, more fine restaurants, more parking lots, more churches—more everything." Not only has the city grown, so has

James City County and the peninsula itself. It is now projected that much of the peninsula will be saturated with population by the year 2040.

Growth accelerated in the Williamsburg area in 1969 when Anheuser-Busch purchased some 3,900 acres from Colonial Williamsburg along the James River. Colonial Williamsburg wanted to look to the future by selling the land to a corporation it believed would take the utmost care in developing commercial, industrial, entertainment, and residential areas. Anheuser-Busch proposed to build a brewery, theme park, and residential development on the acreage. The brewery opened in 1973, Busch Gardens—the Old Country in 1976, and Kingsmill (the name of the development) has been an ongoing planned and gated residential community ever since. Kingsmill set a precedent for attracting residents to the Williamsburg area. With its large lots, preservation of environment, and well-constructed houses, it set an example that similar developments in the area have followed. The idea was to preserve the flavor of Colonial Williamsburg while unprecedented growth took place. In addition, Water Country, USA appeared in the area to provide additional entertainment during summer months. Area economists debate whether the additions of Busch Gardens and Water Country have hurt or helped Colonial Williamsburg's attendance. While attendance charges for all the possible venues in the area seem high, it is possible to buy a year's pass to Colonial Williamsburg for just under $40. The Freedom Pass admits its holder to exhibit buildings and many special events.

With Anheuser-Busch's Kingsmill setting the example, the Williamsburg area was able to control development, keeping the kind of uncontrolled growth that has afflicted so many parts of the nation from proliferating. Kingsmill advertised across the nation for prospective buyers and many came, especially those wishing to retire in the area. Attracted by Colonial Williamsburg's charm, the climate (although summer heat and humidity can be almost unbearable), and a cost of living considerably below national average, many military retirees especially were lured to the area. There are conventional developments, but they exhibit some concern for the environment and the surroundings within which they are set.

An added benefit for James City County from Anheuser-Busch's decision to locate in it was a substantial increase in taxes that the brewery and theme park brought. In 1969, the county had had to ask the city to help defray its share of costs for the jointly-operated school system, but by 1975 it could point to a surplus in its treasury thanks to Anheuser-Busch and its properties. Construction jobs and some 300 permanent jobs in the brewery itself provided further benefits to the community. When Busch Gardens opened in 1976, its seasonal nature opened summer jobs for hundreds of college students home for summer break.

Williamsburg in Modern Times: 1970–2004

Another opportunity to appeal to the nation came in 1976, the bicentennial of the Declaration of Independence and Colonial Williamsburg's own fiftieth birthday. Colonial Williamsburg and the city held a special celebration of those events on July 4, but kept the party going pretty much the whole summer. Reminded again of the importance of the principles of freedom and liberty embedded in the Revolution, those who came to Williamsburg for the commemoration that summer had the opportunity to forget for a few moments the agony the nation had just gone through—Vietnam, the oil crisis, and subsequent inflation that it brought on, and the impeachment and resignation of President Richard M. Nixon.

The foundation used its fiftieth birthday to begin fund raising nationally. A newly-created development office launched the campaign to raise money to help support the educational, research, archaeological, and construction programs ongoing at Colonial Williamsburg. In 2000 the foundation raised almost $47 million to support the work. Sums like that reinforce admission fees, sales from gift shops, hotel and restaurant net incomes, and endowment funds.

In keeping with John D. Rockefeller Jr.'s dedication to the restoration, his family has maintained its presence as active participants in Colonial Williamsburg since his death in 1960. His five sons, especially Winthrop and John D. Rockefeller III, have been very active in the management of the foundation. Grandchildren still participate as directors, members of the board of trustees, advisors, and interested participants in the events and celebrations in the restoration. Another family whose affection for the restoration translated into long-term participation and support is that of Lila and DeWitt Wallace. The Wallaces, founders of Reader's Digest Association, contributed the monies to rebuild the Public Hospital on its original site, before it moved to its present site of Dunbar plantation just to the city's west. Their support for conservation and collection of eighteenth-century artifacts has served an important part of the foundation's mission.

In the meantime, the city and Colonial Williamsburg reinforced their partnership through a widening exploration of the region's history. A partnership in historical archaeology and history has led to an understanding of the early history of the area despite the tragic loss of James City County's public documents in the fire that consumed Richmond at the end of the Civil War. "Digs" conducted by Ivor Noël Hume while director of archaeology for Colonial Williamsburg uncovered during the 1950s to early 1980s not only the below-ground material culture of the city but many parts of the area surrounding the town. His students and colleagues, professional archaeologists like Alain Outlaw, are among the many actively working archaeologists in the area. Professional and local historians alike continue to find new documentary materials or reinterpret from different viewpoints already known materials.

Williamsburg

As the 400th anniversary of the first permanent English settlement at Jamestown approaches, one significant project, called Jamestown Rediscovery, is an archaeological exploration of Jamestown's original fort, located on land owned by the Association for the Preservation of Virginia Antiquities. But all over the county and in the town itself history is one of the defining characteristics, for there are sites dating from prehistoric times through the Civil War, attesting to the historical importance of the Williamsburg area.

During the 1980s and 1990s, many national and world leaders visited the town, including most presidents since Richard Nixon. Jimmy Carter and Gerald Ford held a debate at William and Mary during the 1976 presidential campaign. An economic summit of leaders of the world's strongest economies met in the city in 1983. In 1993, William and Mary commemorated its 300th anniversary and the city did likewise in 1999. The city has retained much of its small town flavor, however.

A town noted for its volunteerism, that trait remains an important element of its character today. The town is economically divided, as many U.S. towns and cities are, between haves and have-nots. Although the city's median income is well above the average for the State of Virginia, there is a substantial amount of poverty in the city; perhaps 10 percent of the city's population exists below the official poverty line and a somewhat larger percentage of the population needs some or a lot of financial help. There are a number of voluntary associations committed to helping those in need. Included are free legal assistance, a free medical clinic, and a group that helps those who need work on their houses.

Williamsburg residents continue to wrestle with the problem of race. Although the percentage of black and white residents in the city remains about the same as it has been historically, the percentage of blacks in James City County is dropping as more and more white people move into the county. But Hispanics and other minority populations continue to grow in the area, making it more heterogeneous than it ever was historically. In the 1970s a black couple came to tour Williamsburg. Unable to obtain accommodations in the Inn or Lodge (both of which were full at the time), they opted to stay in one of the local private guest houses. They were turned away from several because they were African American. The foundation's leadership tried to pressure private guest house owners to open their doors to minorities as a result of such incidents, but it still took a long time for such to occur. The city's institutions, like much of the rest of the peninsula, have opened themselves to all, but neither people, black or white, seems willing to cross what appears to be an invisible racial divide. Regardless of whether the institution is a school or a church or a club, blacks and whites do not seem to mix with each other.

In the 1980s, Colonial Williamsburg set out to make its educational and "on-the-street" presentations of the bi-racial nature of eighteenth-century city society more public. It employed African Americans to present programs such as "The Other Half" that demonstrated how slaves lived, worked, and played in the eighteenth-century city. The intent was to give more authenticity to the Historic Area. By the early 1990s, the foundation felt comfortable enough to try a radical experiment—the reenactment of a slave auction in the city. The public's reaction was one of horror and the condemnation was so strong that the foundation suspended the program. Perhaps the people of the United States are still unready to face the reality of their past.

Churches remain central cultural as well as religious institutions for African Americans in Williamsburg. A variety of black churches, such as St. John Baptist, still provide much of the fabric of life for African Americans in the community. Pastors like Junius Moody are also community leaders, often participating in local politics to represent blacks publicly. Black community leaders want good schools and educations for black children. They fight hard to obtain such, but have residual racism and a series of other problems to face. Other issues that have confronted blacks in town include the Vietnam War and its effects on veterans and their families. Increased use of drugs has created a significant problem in the community as well. Finally, the fragility of family has affected blacks as much as it has whites.

The religious life of Williamsburg has become more and more diverse as the twentieth century ended. Two Presbyterian, two Methodist, three Lutheran, three Episcopal, over twenty Baptist, one Roman Catholic, and one Jewish temple comprise mainstream churches in the Williamsburg area. In addition, there are eight denominational and non-denominational congregations and fellowships including a Christian Science reading room and a Byzantine Catholic Church. There is a growing population of Asians in the Williamsburg area who worship in Eastern faiths; they have to travel to Richmond or Newport News, however, to find places of worship. Eventually, though, there will probably be sites in or around town for them as well.

If the City continues to grow as it has in the last three decades, the problems—especially traffic—it experiences will only mushroom. Vehicular traffic along the city's often narrow streets is very congested at many times during the day, especially in the summer tourist season. Another important traffic problem is the interstate highway system. The construction of the interstate system in the 1950s and 1960s opened the peninsula to more and more auto, bus, and truck traffic along I-64, which connects Newport News and Hampton with Richmond and runs right by Williamsburg. Work on I-64 sometimes seems endless to peninsula residents who are beginning to get the same kind of "rush hour" delays that are found in Washington,

Williamsburg

D.C. or New York City. Heavy traffic at the Busch Gardens exits often slow those who work in Williamsburg but live farther down the peninsula and vice-versa. In the city, despite having closed many streets to vehicular traffic, there are still many vehicles, both those owned by residents and those owned by tourists. The city government has enacted laws to try to control traffic and parking, but it still helps to know the back streets and shortcuts to get around the town if one has lots of errands to run.

To provide visitors plenty to occupy their attention, Colonial Williamsburg has broadened its programs. The Fourth of July, Christmas, Thanksgiving, George Washington's birthday, and many other holidays have special remembrances in the Restored Area. Among visitors' favorite forms of entertainment during these celebrations is the Fife and Drum Corps. Composed of boys and girls from the town, the corps has become one of the official symbols of Colonial Williamsburg, participating in parades and giving demonstrations nationally. Boys and girls must retire from the corps when they reach their eighteenth birthday, but they remain alumni of the corps for the rest of their lives. Bonds of friendship are formed among corps members and some alumni remain part of Colonial Williamsburg as employees long after their service in the corps.

Other holiday ceremonies that combine town and Colonial Williamsburg are the Grand Illumination, during which the town in early December begins its Christmas festival with an official lighting of electric (originally wax) candles in street-facing windows. The town crier walks through the town on Grand Illumination night crying to all the occupants to light their lights. The town's windows remain alight at night through the Christmas and New Year's celebrations. In the Tucker house the foundation re-erects each Christmas season a replica of the first Christmas tree in the room in which Charles Minnegerode placed it back in the 1840s.

The colonial militia also participates in Colonial Williamsburg festivities. It provides cannon demonstrations on Courthouse Green during those celebrations. The cannon noise can be heard for miles, and the first time newcomers hear them they think that some terrible explosion has occurred.

With the reconstruction of the Restored Area complete, Colonial Williamsburg has embarked on an extensive program of maintenance. Original buildings are approximately 250 to 300 years old and need constant attention. Those reconstructed are in many cases seventy to seventy-five years of age. Wear and tear from daily visitors, often numbering in the hundreds or even near a thousand, necessitates substantial amounts of investment in curation and preservation. Similarly, the vast collection of artifacts that Colonial Williamsburg has acquired needs protection.

These too are costly and time consuming. There are still outbuildings on many town lots that have not been reconstructed and the foundation intends to find archaeologically and rebuild as many as possible. These include kitchens, dairies, wash houses, and stables, for example. As their sites and footprints are found, they will be placed on the reconstruction list.

One of the central themes of a history of the City of Williamsburg is history, its facts, analysis, and interpretation. How history is used forms the core of the modern-day city, just as the eighteenth-century city made history. In one sense that use may be placed in the service of dreams and nostalgia, for as Dr. Goodwin himself put it:

> There are thousands of cities in this country with Main Streets, but only one with a Duke of Gloucester Street like ours. There are many Protestant Churches, but none so long conspicuously in use as Bruton Parish . . . when you walk around Williamsburg late on a moonlight night you can see the Indians on the Court Green, where they used to meet to make their treaties of peace . . . and you can see the agents of old Lord Dunmore, stealing the powder out of the Powder Horn, and you can hear the rattle of the horses' hoofs coming down the Richmond Road as Patrick Henry and the Hanover Volunteers rode on to Williamsburg and demanded the powder be restored.

In another sense, the past and history may be used to inform the present and to prepare for the future. As Colonial Williamsburg Foundation President Colin G. Campbell recently phrased it:

> We have more to convey than the classic historical message of how and why revolution came to America. We in Williamsburg have the opportunity to deal with the critical issues of the past that continue to dominate our present—questions of race, religion, gender, civics, and participation in the political process—and in doing so, make a significant contribution to America's future. Colonial Williamsburg is not only about yesterday. It is about the impact of yesterday on today and on tomorrow.

SUGGESTED READING

Andrews, Matthew Page. *Virginia: The Old Dominion*. Reprint edition. Richmond, VA: The Dietz Press, (1949), 1956.

Bath, Gerald Horton. *America's Williamsburg: Why and How the historic Capital of Virginia, oldest and largest of England's Thirteen American Colonies, has been Restored to its Eighteenth Century appearance by John D. Rockefeller, Jr.* Williamsburg: Colonial Williamsburg, Inc., 1954.

Belvin, Ed. *Growing Up in Williamsburg: From the Depression to Pearl Harbor*. Revised edition. n.c.: Graphic Impressions, 2003.

————. *Williamsburg: Facts & Fiction, 1900–1950*. n.c.: Printwell, Inc., n.d.

Beverley, Robert. *The History and Present State of Virginia*. Chapel Hill, NC: University of North Carolina Press for the [Omohundro] Institute of Early American History and Culture, 1947.

Bowie, Beverley M. "Williamsburg: Its College and Its Cinderella City." Reprint from *National Geographic Magazine*, Vol. CVI, No. 4 (Oct. 1954), Washington, D.C.: National Geographic, 1954.

Craven, Wesley Frank. *The Southern Colonies in the Seventeenth Century, 1607–1689. A History of the South* series, volume II. Baton Rouge, LA: Louisiana State University Press for the Littlefield Fund for Southern History of the University of Texas, 1970.

Chesapeake & Ohio Railway. *Visit Colonial Williamsburg with Us*. n.c.: C&O Travel Service, 1941.

"Directory and Handbook of the City of Williamsburg and the County of James City, Virginia." Williamsburg: *The Virginia Gazette*, 1898.

Dubbs, Carol Kettenburg. "Fortress Williamsburg: Treasure Through Four Years of War." *Williamsburg, Virginia: A City Before the State, 1699–1999*. Williamsburg: 300th Anniversary Commission, 2000.

Edwards, Jack. "Change and Growth: Williamsburg Begins a Fourth Century." *Williamsburg, Virginia: A City Before the State, 1699–1999*. Williamsburg: 300th Anniversary Commission, 2000.

Ewing, William C. *The Sports of Colonial Williamsburg*. Richmond, VA: The Dietz Press, 1937.

Foster, Andrea Kim. " 'They're Turning the Town All Upside Down.' " Ph.D. dissertation: George Washington University, 1993.

Foster, Mary L. *Colonial Capitals of the Dominion of Virginia*. Lynchburg, VA: J.P. Bell, Inc., 1906.

Williamsburg

Goodwin, Rutherfoord. *A Brief & True Report Concerning Williamsburg in Virginia: Being an Account . . . to Which is added an Appendix composed of the Records. . . .* Richmond, VA: August Dietz & Son for Colonial Williamsburg, 1940.

Goodwin, Rev. Wm. A.R. *Bruton Parish Church: Restored and its Historic Environment.* Petersburg, VA: The Franklin Press, 1907.

Greenspan, Anders. *Creating Colonial Williamsburg.* Washington, D.C.: Smithsonian Institution Press, 2002.

Handler, Richard, and Eric Gable. *The New History in an Old Museum: Creating the Past at Colonial Williamsburg.* Durham, NC: Duke University Press, 1997.

Hawthorne, Hildegarde. *Williamsburg: Old and New.* New York: D. Appleton-Century Company, 1941.

Hudson, Carter O. Jr. *Civil War Williamsburg.* Williamsburg: Colonial Williamsburg Foundation in association with Stackpole Books, Mechanicsburg, PA, 1997.

Isaac, Rhys. *The Transformation of Virginia, 1740–1790.* New York: The University of North Carolina Press for the (Omohundro) Institute of Early American History and Culture, 1982.

Jones, Hugh. *The Present State of Virginia; From Whence is Inferred a Short View of Maryland and North Carolina.* Chapel Hill, NC: Published for the Virginia Historical Society by the University of North Carolina Press, 1956.

Maccubbin, Robert P., ed. *Williamsburg, Virginia: A City Before the State, 1699–1999* Commissioned and produced by Martha Hamilton-Phillips, 300th Anniversary Commission. Williamsburg: The City of Williamsburg, 2000.

McCartney, Martha. *James City County: Keystone of the Commonwealth.* Virginia Beach, VA: The Donning Company Publishers, 1997.

Noël Hume, Ivor. *Archaeology and Wetherburn's Tavern.* Williamsburg: Colonial Williamsburg, Inc., 1969.

———. *James Geddy and Sons: Colonial Craftsmen.* Williamsburg: Colonial Williamsburg, Inc., 1970.

Osborne, Joseph Alexander. *Williamsburg in Colonial Times.* Richmond, VA: The Dietz Press, Publishers, 1925.

Osborne, Marian. *Anne's Letters: Readings with the Author, through many of the Historic Places in Colonial Williamsburg in Virginia.* Williamsburg: The Virginia Gazette, n.d.

Oxrieder, Julia Woodbridge. *Rich, Black, and Southern: The Harris Family of Williamsburg (and Boston).* New Church, VA: Mione Publications, 1998.

———. "Williamsburg Claims the Amenities of Life, 1880–1920." *Williamsburg, Virginia: A City Before the State, 1699–1999.* Williamsburg: 300th Anniversary Commission, 2000.

Poag, C. Wylie. *Chesapeake Invader: Discovering America's Giant Meteorite Crater.* Princeton, NJ: Princeton University Press, 1999.

Powers, Emma L. " 'No mean city': Antebellum Williamsburg." *Williamsburg, Virginia: A City Before the State, 1699–1999.* Williamsburg: 300th Anniversary Commission, 2000.

Suggested Reading

Reps, John William. *Tidewater Towns: City Planning in Colonial Virginia and Maryland.* Williamsburg: The Colonial Williamsburg Foundation, 1972.

Rountree, Helen. *Pocahontas's People: The Powhatan Indians of Virginia Through Four Centuries.* Norman, OK: University of Oklahoma Press, 1990.

Rouse, Parke Jr. *The City That Turned Back Time: Colonial Williamsburg's First Twenty-Five Years.* Second printing. Williamsburg: Colonial Williamsburg, Inc., 1962.

————. *Cows on the Campus: Williamsburg in Bygone Days.* Richmond, VA: The Dietz Press, 1973.

————. *Remembering Williamsburg: A Sentimental Journey Through Three Centuries.* Richmond, Va.: The Dietz Press, 1989.

Rowe, Linda. "African Americans in Williamsburg, 1865–1945." *Williamsburg, Virginia: A City Before the State, 1699–1999.* Williamsburg: 300th Anniversary Commission, 2000.

Stevens, William Oliver. *Old Williamsburg and Her Neighbors.* New York: Dodd, Mead & Co., 1938.

Tate, Thad W. *The Negro in Eighteenth-Century Williamsburg.* Williamsburg: The Colonial Williamsburg Foundation, 1965.

Tate, Thaddeus W. Jr. "Town and Gown Through Three Centuries: William & Mary in the Life of Williamsburg." *Williamsburg, Virginia: A City Before the State, 1699–1999.* Williamsburg: 300th Anniversary Commission, 2000.

Taylor, Thomas H. Jr. "The Restoration of Williamsburg." *Williamsburg, Virginia: A City Before the State, 1699–1999.* Williamsburg: 300th Anniversary Commission, 2000.

Theobald, Mary Miley. *Colonial Williamsburg: The First 75 Years.* Williamsburg: The Colonial Williamsburg Foundation, 2001.

Turner, John. "Three Hundred Years of Faith," *Williamsburg, Virginia: A City Before the State, 1699–1999.* Williamsburg: 300th Anniversary Commission, 2000.

Tuttle, Jackson C. II. "From Oligarchy to Democracy: Governing Virginia's First City." *Williamsburg, Virginia: A City Before the State, 1699–1999.* Williamsburg: 300th Anniversary Commission, 2000.

Tyler, Lyon G. "Williamsburg—The Old Colonial Capital." *William and Mary Quarterly*, 1st Series, Vol. XVI, No. 1 (July, 1907), pp. 1–65.

————. *Williamburg: The Old Colonial Capital.* Williamsburg: College of William and Mary, 1928.

Williamsburg Garden Club, The. *A Williamsburg Scrap Book.* Richmond, VA: The Dietz Press, 1950.

Yetter, George Humphrey. *Williamsburg Before and After: The Rebirth of Virginia's Colonial Capital.* Williamsburg: The Colonial Williamsburg Foundation, Inc., 1988.

INDEX

Index